THE RESTLESS EVIL

A Play

CHARLOTTE HASTINGS

SAMUEL   FRENCH

LONDON
NEW YORK   TORONTO   SYDNEY   HOLLYWOOD

© 1977 BY CHARLOTTE HASTINGS

This play is fully protected under the copyright laws of the British Commonwealth of Nations, the United States of America, and all countries of the Berne and Universal Copyright Conventions.

All rights are strictly reserved.

It is an infringement of the copyright to give any public performance or reading of this play either in its entirety or in the form of excerpts without the prior consent of the copyright owners. No part of this publication may be transmitted, stored in a retrieval system, or reproduced in any form or by any means, electronic, mechanical, photocopying, manuscript, typescript, recording, or otherwise, without the prior permission of the copyright owners.

SAMUEL FRENCH LTD, 26 SOUTHAMPTON STREET, STRAND, LONDON WC2E 7JE, or their authorized agents, issue licences to amateurs to give performances of this play on payment of a fee. **The fee must be paid and the licence obtained before a performance is given.**

Licences are issued subject to the understanding that it shall be made clear in all advertising matter that the audience will witness an amateur performance; and that the names of the authors of the plays shall be included on all announcements and on all programmes.

The royalty fee indicated below is subject to contract and subject to variation at the sole discretion of Samuel French Ltd.

The publication of this play must not be taken to imply that it is necessarily available for performance by amateurs or professionals, either in the British Isles or overseas. Amateurs intending production must, in their own interests, make application to Samuel French Ltd or their authorized agents, for consent before starting rehearsals or booking a theatre or hall.

Basic fee for each and every
performance by amateurs   Code K
in the British Isles

In theatres or halls seating 600 or more the fee will be subject to negotiation.

In territories overseas the fee quoted above may not apply. Application must be made to our local authorized agents, or if there is no such agent, to Samuel French Ltd, London.

ISBN 0 573 11370 X

MADE AND PRINTED IN GREAT BRITAIN BY
LATIMER TREND & COMPANY LTD PLYMOUTH
MADE IN ENGLAND

THE RESTLESS EVIL

CHARACTERS

Linamacoola (Lina)
Jubilee
Joe
Clem
Julia Sanders-King
Mrs Phyllis Stevens
Mrs Brockett
Hester Davenport
Reverend Henry Cole
Matty Fisher

The action takes place in the Prospect Café, a small café in a by-road off a motorway in the West Country

ACT I
   Scene 1   Saturday noon
   Scene 2   About an hour later

ACT II   An hour later

ACT III   An hour later

Time—the present

PRODUCTION NOTE

Basically, this play contains a static situation, six people immobilized in a small space by three gunmen.

Detailed stage directions have therefore been given, designed to keep a constant flow of movement across the stage, and to bring everyone to the right place at the right time, particularly where the dialogue fades from one group and is taken up by another. If producers will follow these directions, it will be found that a correct pattern evolves, the action changes with the mood—and also a great amount of time will be saved at rehearsals.

SING FOR PLEASURE is a real organization, an association of choirs in the United Kingdom, with wide representation abroad and sponsored by the Standing Conference for Amateur Music. All references to it, and all situations arising from it in the context of the play, must be taken seriously. Voices of operatic standard are not required, but the two small singing episodes should be done tunefully and quietly. Societies may use another carol instead of "Holy Night", and anyone ambitious enough may try a simple round or catch such as "London's Burning" or "Frère Jacques", which would be particularly interesting. If Julia prefers, she may speak the words from *Judas Maccabaeus* in Act III instead of singing them. These interludes of music must not be cut. They are important in the context and also as lighter moments in a grim situation.

As the guns are not fired, this obviates the complication of hiring under licence. Toy guns may be used effectively and are small enough to be pocketed easily.

No cuts or alterations to the dialogue or characters of this play may be made without reference to, or permission from, Samuel French Ltd.

ACT I

Scene 1

The Prospect Café, a small café in a by-road off a motorway in the West Country. Saturday noon

The café has painted walls decorated with trade advertisements. The back wall is filled by large plate-glass windows, slightly recessed to make a sill with pots of red geraniums: the words "PROSPECT CAFÉ" are visible in reverse across the top, with an Open/Closed sign hung below the name. The window looks out on a pull-in courtyard bordered by trees. There is a windowseat running the length of the window, upholstered in red. Long curtains can be run across it, striped in red and yellow, under a matching scalloped pelmet. There is a small radio on the window sill. There are two doors: a main one, and, opposite it, one to the interior of the house. The furnishings are of modern design—red-topped bar stools, a chrome and plastic table with stacking chairs round it, counter, etc. (See Furniture and Property List and plan of set on page 60)

When the CURTAIN *rises the notice in the window is turned to read "OPEN", and the radio is playing. Motorcycles are heard approaching. Three figures in leather gear pass the window. Impatient hammering is heard on the main door*

Lina (*off*) All right—all right . . .

Lina enters from the interior, yawning, a slim West Indian about twenty-five, gay red overall, sandals, turban-type scarf on her head, hoop gold earrings

The knocking continues

(*Crossing*) I'm coming—I'm coming. Man, you sure are in a hurry. (*She turns the sign to read "CLOSED" and flicks off the radio in passing*) Didn't you see closed sign? (*She pulls back the top bolt and opens the main door*)

Jubilee rushes in, gun in hand, stifling Lina's scream

Jubilee pulls Lina round against him, his left hand round her neck and over her mouth, and rams her against the counter, bent over, gun in her ribs. Distant police sirens are heard, coming nearer. Jubilee is forty-five, big, powerful and with short dark hair. He wears a black leather jacket and pants, pink shirt, and a round dark blue cap with a leather peak. He is usually morose, but articulate, even dangerous, when roused

Enter Joe, slim, twenty-five, in one-piece leather overalls and yellow crash-helmet, walking quickly and lightly, like a cat. Joe goes straight to the door, pauses, suddenly kicks it open and darts through. Clem enters last, bolts the door and stands with his back against it. He is twenty-four, tall, good-looking, dark hair rather long. He wears leather gear but is bareheaded. He has a pleasant, educated voice and considerable charm. They all carry small hand guns

The siren comes nearer. Lina makes a stifled sound. Jubilee presses the gun harder in her back

Jubilee (*in a low voice*) Shut it . . .!

A pause. The siren comes nearer, passes and fades

> *Joe enters, makes a thumbs-up sign, and turns the window notice to read "OPEN"*

Clem No-one? No-one at all?

Joe shakes head, goes behind the counter, finds some mugs and uses the Cona. Clem sits at the table, pocketing his gun

> Well, well.

Jubilee Bit of flaming luck.
Clem (*pleasantly*) Flaming. So let her go.
Jubilee Eh?

Joe makes a hissing noise to attract Clem

Joe S-s-ss . . . (*Takes a pack of cigarettes from the shelf and tosses it across to Clem*)
Clem Thanks. Let her go, Jube. We want to know the set-up.

Joe cracks open the till with the gun butt, and counts out three small piles of notes on the counter

Jubilee (*to Lina*) So listen, sister. You answer a few questions and no-one'll hurt you, Right?

Lina nods

> Damned wog.

Jubilee pushes her towards Clem, who jumps up and steadies her. Jubilee goes to the counter for coffee

Clem Easy there. Come and sit down.

Clem takes her to a chair at the table. He sits in another chair below the table, offering the cigarettes to her

> Here—have a fag.

Her hand shakes too much

> Oh, come on—this won't do . . . (*He puts a cigarette in her mouth*) Coffee, Joe.

Act I, Scene 1

Clem lights Lina's cigarette. Joe fills two mugs and pushes them towards Jubilee. He scowls, but takes the mugs in one hand to the table. He stands drinking his own coffee

Drink that while it's hot. Better? Good. Now—question one. Are you the owner?

Lina shakes her head

Question two. Who is?

Jubilee And question three and question four—where the hell are they, and are they coming back?

Clem All *right*, Jube. One thing at a time. (*To Lina*) Best to be sensible.

Lina (*sullenly*) Mr and Mrs Marshall. They're away in London. But they'll be back...

Clem When?

Lina (*in a rush*) I tole you—they gone to London. They leave me in charge. Now you go—all of you—you got the money. Now you go leave us in peace...

Jubilee When will they be back?

Lina does not answer

When?

She still does not answer. Jubilee steps forward, raising his hand

Clem (*quietly*) No, Jube.
Jubilee She'd better answer.
Clem She will. Won't you, love?
Lina Monday morning.
Jubilee Closed for the week-end. I said flaming luck. (*He goes back to a stool*) Stupid wog.
Lina (*flaring up*) Who you calling stupid! There's a special party comin' for lunch. Six! And they'll get you. So you go now—you great hulking lump!

Jubilee puts his mug on the counter and comes forward, head lowered

Clem (*warningly*) Jube...
Jubilee She called me...
Clem You called her a stupid wog. She called you a hulking brute. That makes you quits...
Jubilee It makes me flaming mad...
Joe S-s-ss...

Jubilee turns. Joe holds up the wad of notes. Jubilee goes back to the stool, takes the notes and counts them

Clem So what's this about a party?
Lina Friends of Mr Marshall's. They're going on somewhere. Some meeting. They ordered lunch.
Jubilee So when they get here it's closed. They knock. They get no answer. They go away. Easy.

Lina They don't go. They'll be suspicious. They telephone ten o'clock this morning to make sure I'm ready . . .

Clem Six people? You're certain?

Lina 'Course I'm certain. They been before—at least the priest man has . . .

Jubilee Priest man? You mean a Jesus freak? Crissake, that's all we need. She's right. We've got the cash. What are we waiting for . . . (*He pockets the notes and stands up*)

Clem Hang about. Joe, find somewhere in the back where we can shut her up for a bit.

Joe takes out the gun and moves behind Lina

Lina No—you don't do that . . .

Clem Only for a minute or two, love. Just while we sort things out.

Joe takes Lina off inside

Jubilee looks after them, then returns to the middle of the room

Jubilee He gives me the creeps. Who is he?

Clem The one who got you away.

Jubilee No, he flaming didn't. That was Baron. And he fixed it with Spikey Adams. When I was over the wall I was to meet you. We'd been running half an hour before he turned up. Quite sudden. There he was. In the dark. With the bikes. Uncanny.

Clem Listen, Jube . . .

Jubilee He isn't one of Spikey's old lot. Not that I know of . . .

Clem Four years is a long time. Things change. And people.

Jubilee Spikey wouldn't change that way. He wasn't ever one for boys. (*Laughing*) No, by God. Not Spikey. Not boys. So who's this little zombie?

Clem A specialist. Knows every whichway and backway in this part of England. Forty-eight hours—we'll be safe to the coast.

Jubilee O.K. So he's the Lone Star Ranger. So why doesn't he speak? I know he can—I've seen him talking to you. But to me, not a word——

Clem Look . . .

Jubilee —not a flaming word. And a face—what you can see of it—like a split flint. Like I said—he gives me the creeps——

Clem Calm down, Jube. It's been a long night. You're tired . . .

Jubilee I'm tired of being talked down by you. You're the one that's changed. Why? Because you're educated? Educated—where's it got you, anyway. I never had education——

Joe enters

—and right now I know where there's more money than you'll ever see in your educated little life . . .

Joe speaks suddenly in a cold clear voice

Joe Jubilee.

Act I, Scene 1

Jubilee and Clem turn

Cool it.
Jubilee Why...
Joe I said cool it.

Joe removes the helmet, shaking out a mane of long blonde hair, and revealing a girl, self-possessed, and attractive, in spite of the thin features and cold smile

Well, do I still give you the creeps?

Clem laughs

Jubilee Flaming hell. (*To Clem*) Why didn't you tell me?
Joe Because I said not to. (*She puts her helmet on the windowseat and comes down, still with the gun*) All right, Clem. Leave it to me now...?
Clem Sure, Joe. Whatever you say. (*He sits back, amused, lighting a cigarette*)
Jubilee What *is* this? *You* say—*you* take over. Where do you come in—oh, yes. I said Spikey wouldn't change. So that's it. Well, he always did know how to pick 'em...
Joe (*coolly*) I don't belong to Spikey. I work for him. Like you. Like Clem. Our job was to help you get out. You *are* out—out and free. I understand you're complaining?
Jubilee I'm not complaining. I just want to get on with it. What's the plan?
Joe We keep together. We meet Spikey in Barnstaple. You show us where you hid the cash and we collect. We make for the coast. No hitch, by Monday we're in Spain. For now—we wait here...
Jubilee Wait—wait! I've been waiting four years.
Joe Long enough to learn patience. (*She pockets her gun and goes to the counter for a mug of coffee*)
Jubilee Patience? You ever been inside?
Joe Never, if I can avoid it.
Jubilee I wait, I get restless. I get restless, something happens.
Joe In forty-eight hours, you can have all the happenings you want... (*She suddenly looks at her wristwatch. She goes to the radio*) Wait...
Jubilee Wait—wait. There you go again...
Joe It's just twelve. Listen... (*She switches on the radio*)
Announcer's Voice ... the Prime Minister stated that unless a firm stand were taken, the country might well face another crisis. (*Pause*) A nationwide police operation has been mounted after the escape early this morning from Colnbrook Prison of John Kevin Jubilee, aged forty-five. Jubilee had served four years of a ten-year sentence in connection with the famous Alton affair, when three men held up a security van, injured a guard and escaped with four hundred thousand pounds. Jubilee and Alan Clement Prior were arrested a week later. Neither the third man nor the money were subsequently traced. Prior was released a year ago after serving two years. Reports have been received that Jubilee was seen in the Gresford area. He is thought to be armed

and the public are warned that he is dangerous. (*Pause*) This morning at London Airport, the actress——

Joe switches off

Jubilee Gresford. That's twenty miles back. We've slipped them. We can get going now . . .
Joe It could be a police trap. We could land slap in a road block. Besides, if we go now, we're travelling in daylight.
Clem Sighting that police car was a bit of bad luck.
Joe Finding this place was a bit of good luck. Win a trick, lose a trick. So long as you win the last.
Jubilee You talk too much.
Joe You don't have to listen——
Jubilee Too right . . .
Joe —but if you don't, you're on your own.
Jubilee (*quietly*) I've played it alone before.
Joe This time you need papers and you need a passport. Spikey's got them. And without us you don't know exactly where he is.
Jubilee And without me, you don't know exactly where there's four hundred thousand pounds.
Joe That's why you're out.

Joe and Jubilee face each other—the battle of wills. Then Jubilee sits on the stool at the upstage end of the counter. He takes out his gun and rests it on his knee

Jubilee (*quietly*) Couple of flaming kids. Spikey must be getting old. All right. But just remember. They said—dangerous. So what comes next?
Joe Either we lock up here, and get away now . . .
Jubilee Like I said.
Joe Like you said. And we know the risks of that.
Jubilee So . . . ?
Joe So we go into the restaurant business.

Clem starts to laugh

Jubilee We flaming what . . . ?
Joe We receive this party. We give them lunch. All normal and cosy. Two casual customers at the counter. They finish their meal. They pay. They go. We hole up here till we're ready. Food, drinks, a radio—it's a honey.
Jubilee Two casual customers . . . ?
Joe You and me.
Jubilee And him?
Joe He'll be mine host.
Jubilee And what does that mean?
Joe Owners are away for the week-end. But they've booked in a lunch party. So they get extra help. They get a graduate on holiday. How about it, Clem?
Clem (*laughing*) I like it, I like it.
Jubilee Well, I flaming don't.

Act I, Scene 1

Joe Clem serves the meal, with that girl, of course. So he keeps an eye on her, charms the customers, and we split all tips three ways. (*To Clem*) Get the girl back. She's locked in the storeroom. (*She takes a bunch of keys from her pocket and gives them to him*) I took her keys.

Clem, laughing, exits to the interior

Jubilee I still don't like it . . .
Joe Better get the bikes hidden. Must be some outbuildings around.

Jubilee pockets his gun, goes to the main door and unbolts it. Joe moves to the wall menu

And cheer up. We'll make it. Remember, the devil looks after his own.
Jubilee (*grimly*) He'd flaming better.

Jubilee goes out by the main door. Clem returns with Lina

Lina sees Joe and gasps. Joe reads from the menu

Joe Steak with french fried. Cod with french fried. Steak, tomatoes and onions with french fried. Cod, peas and french fried. Bacon and tomatoes, with or without french fried. Ice-cream, coffee . . . (*Turning*) And what out of all this are you giving them for lunch?
Lina (*sullenly*) Special order. Cold chicken. Salad. Trifle. Ice-cream. Coffee.
Joe Sounds like a kids' birthday. How long will it take you?
Lina I got it ready in fridge.
Joe Good. And what about—by the way, what's your name?
Lina Linamacoola. I'm called Lina.
Joe I should hope so. Well, Lina, what are you giving them to drink? This place licensed?
Lina No. Mr Cole—he the priest man—he usually brings a bottle of wine.
Joe Bravo, Mr Cole. No alcohol here at all?
Lina Mr Marshall—he got some bottles whisky and brandy of his own.
Joe Whisky . . .

Joe and Clem exchange a glance

Where is it?
Lina Kitchen cupboard.
Joe Does it lock?
Lina (*sullenly*) You got all the keys.

Clem holds up the bunch, then tosses it to Joe

Joe All very neat. Back door, front door, toilet, storeroom—drinks cupboard . . . (*She tosses the bunch back to Clem*) Make sure. Spikey did warn us.

Clem exits to the interior

Now listen carefully, Linamawhatsit. When these people arrive, you'll serve their lunch——

Lina But I...

Joe —you'll behave perfectly naturally. You'll explain that your boss is away. He's taken on Clem to help you. Clem is a graduate on holiday. I suppose you understand that?

Lina I know 'bout graduates.

Joe Good. When they've gone, we'll shut ourselves up here, probably till tomorrow night. Then we'll put you in the storeroom back there...

Lina You can't shut me up...

Joe Stop moaning. It's well ventilated. You'll have food and drink. And on Monday morning you'll have your moment of glory. (*Laughing*) Probably get your name in the papers.

Lina You're *wicked*.

Joe That's right, sweetie. Now, repeat what I said.

Lina I serve lunch. I say that one's a graduate helping out. I behave ordinary. (*Suddenly*) And if the papers talk to me, I tell them you're a bitch!

Joe You do that. What time are these people coming?

Lina Lunch twelve forty-five.

Joe Then we'd better start.

Clem enters, throws the bunch of keys to Joe and goes out again

Joe puts the keys in her overall pocket

Where's the stuff?

Lina (*shortly*) Cutlery ready under counter.

Joe goes to the counter. Lina goes to the table, takes a duster from her pocket, wipes the table, replaces the duster, and returns behind the counter as Joe moves down from the counter with a tray of cutlery. Lina finds a checked cloth under the counter, returns and spreads the cloth. She and Joe lay the table in hostile silence

Jubilee returns and bolts the door

Jubilee Bikes stowed.

Joe Good. Get something on the radio. Something classy. And switch that sign.

Jubilee turns the sign to read "CLOSED" then fiddles with the radio. Lina fetches a small tray with glasses and red paper napkins from the counter to the table. Joe picks up a fork, shakes her head, takes the duster from Lina's pocket, cleans the fork and tosses back the duster. Lina scowls

Announcer's Voice ... In the "Science Today" programme at eight forty-five, Professor Luckin will discuss the mating habits of the Tibetan Corpus beetle in which the male immobilizes the female by covering her with a glutinous secretion...

Joe Jube—for God's sake...

Act I, Scene 1

Jubilee (*laughing*) Thought it sounded sexy . . . (*He switches to music and turns it down softly*)

Joe surveys the table, goes to the window and picks off a geranium which she puts in a glass on the table. Lina scowls and fetches another glass from under the counter to replace it

Clem enters from inside

Clem Last orders, ladies and gentleman, please!

Clem has removed his leather coat, retied his tie, smoothed his hair and wears a blue and white striped jacket. Joe gives a mocking slow handclap

Lina (*indignantly*) You got Mr Marshall's jacket!
Clem Not a bad fit, is it?

Clem inspects the table. Jubilee sits on the upstage stool of the counter. Joe goes to him

Joe Open your jacket—open it wide. And your shirt.

Jubilee does so

That's better. Now remember, we've dropped in for coffee—or perhaps a Coke . . .
Jubilee Coke!
Joe You don't have to drink it. But if you do—use a glass—not from the tin. We answer if we're spoken to, but don't start a conversation. Right?
Jubilee Right.
Joe Get a fag going—helps your hands. They shouldn't stay more than an hour, but we could go outside once, perhaps. (*To Lina*) Where's the gents?
Lina Outside. On left.
Clem There's a car . . .

They pause, listening

Joe It's going by.

Joe collects her helmet and exits to the interior

Clem and Jubilee watch at the window

Jubilee It's passed. She said six people. That'll mean more than one car . . .

Lina edges backwards round the table. She makes a sudden dive for the main door. Jubilee is too quick, he grabs her as she touches the handle

Crazy little fool—what do you think you're doing? (*He pushes her against the table, bringing out his gun*) If you try *one* thing—mind, just *one* thing—while they're here—someone will get hurt. And whoever it is, it'll be your fault. Got it?

Lina nods

I should hope so. Now you be doing something to that table . . .
Clem Here's a car—they're coming . . .
Jubilee (*to Lina*) And when they get here—smile. (*He pockets his gun and joins Clem at the window*) That's going by, too. No, it isn't—crissake, look at that. A bloody great old Daimler. Must be vintage. Cor—if I could get my hands on that . . .

Joe enters and goes to the downstage stool. She has removed her overalls; she now wears light blue jeans and a white tailored shirt, her hair is tied back in a neat ponytail. She is putting the gun in her big hip pocket

Clem turns, sees her and goes to her

Clem (*smiling*) "Shall I compare thee to a summer's day—?"

He kisses her. She returns the kiss, then half-laughing, half-serious, pushes him away

Joe Oh, get off . . .

Jubilee returns to the counter

Jubilee So that's how it is . . .
Joe Yes, Jube. That's how it is.

A car is heard to arrive and stop

(*To Clem*) Go and meet them. Do your stuff.

Clem gives the thumbs-up sign, settles his jacket and crosses to the main door. He makes a warning sign to Lina, and goes out

Joe leans back on the stool, stretching out her legs

Joe So you've got a girl-friend, Jubilee. How do you like it?
Jubilee (*softly*) I like it. After four years—I like it very much.

He presses hard against her. Joe puts both hands on his chest and stops him

Joe (*very quietly*) Watch it—lover-boy . . .

Jubilee moves back to the stool. They sit looking at each other. Something like hatred passes between them

Clem (*off*) Good morning, sir. Good morning, ladies. We're all ready for you. Please come in . . .

CURTAIN

SCENE 2

The same. An hour later

Five of the party are sitting round the table. Henry Cole at the upstage end, on his R in that order: Hester Davenport, Julia Sanders-King, Mrs Stevens and at the downstage end Mrs Brockett. Matty Fisher sits on the window-seat. She has a big shoulder-bag beside her and is reading a book with her glasses on. Henry is about thirty-eight, well built. He wears a summer clerical outfit, light grey with grey silk pleated vest and clerical collar. Hester Davenport is sixty, elegant, white hair smartly styled. She has a gentle cultured voice. Mrs King is big, stocky, fifty-odd, short hair. She wears a lightweight tweed suit. She has a booming voice and is inclined to steam-roller people. Mrs Brockett is a small thin woman in her seventies, shrewd and quite fearless. She wears a cotton dress and sensible shoes; a light cardigan is draped over the back of her chair. Mrs Stevens is forty, slight and drooping with a worried expression and a high plaintive voice. Matty is very intelligent, twenty, pretty, in a casual summer dress

As the CURTAIN *rises, they are discussing a music score spread over the table. Lina is just turning away with their used dishes and cutlery on a tray. Joe and Jubilee are still on their stools. Clem is waiting by the inner door. As Lina goes out with the tray he follows her*

Julia No, no. If you *scoop* it like that it'll be one long *drone* . . . (*She sings in a good soprano, beating time*) "Haste, haste, shepherds and neighbours"—come along, from the beginning.

The group sing the first verse through.* Jubilee casts up his eyes and takes a drink

"—at the end of the d-a-y."

Julia cuts them off with a flourish

That's better. Much better. Now, Phyllis, do you think you've got it?
Mrs Stevens (*anxiously*) Yes. I think so. It's not actually the *music* . . .
Julia Then what is it?
Mrs Stevens It's—it's when you give the signal—and everyone stands up *suddenly*—(*her voice rises*)—I get *nervous* . . .
Julia What nonsense.
Mrs Brockett If this thing's called "Sing for Pleasure" she's not a very good advertisement for it.
Mrs Stevens It's all very well for you. You don't know what nerves mean . . .
Mrs Brockett I've had ten children and reared eight. What time does that leave for nerves?
Henry Don't worry, Julia. We shan't let you down. And it's not competitive.
Julia Just as well. I haven't forgotten that time when the scores got mixed. Half of them singing "Oh that We Two were Maying" and the other half belting out the "Alleluia Chorus". I still dream about it.
Hester Well, I do think attempting oratorio is just a little bit ambitious.
Julia Rubbish. We want to *stretch* ourselves. Got to try something before we know we can't do it.
Henry (*laughing*) Better to fail gloriously . . .

* See Production Note.

Mrs Stevens (*dolefully*) But it wouldn't be glorious—I mean to fail—would it?
Mrs Brockett Lord give me patience. (*She goes to the counter and opens her handbag*)

Lina returns, and goes behind the counter

Twenty tipped Woods, please.

Lina serves her from the shelves, and puts the money in the till drawer

Thanks. Hullo—what's happened to your till?
Lina I—I lost the key.
Mrs Brockett Careless. I thought you'd had vandals. (*She sits on the seat by Matty*)

Clem enters from inside with a tray and goes to the table

Clem More coffee, ladies and gentlemen?
Henry No, thank you.

Clem clears the cups

That was a very good meal.
Clem Glad you enjoyed it, sir. (*He turns to go*)
Henry How are Mr and Mrs Marshall?
Clem (*turning back*) Very well, thank you, sir. They were sorry to miss you.
Henry They left us in excellent hands. Lina tells me you're a graduate.
Clem That's right, sir. Just helping out.

Clem turns and moves towards the counter. Matty speaks as he passes

Matty Where were you?
Clem (*turning*) I beg your pardon, Miss?

Lina takes the tray from Clem and exits inside

Joe looks at Jubilee

Jubilee gets up and follows Lina off

Matty University . . . ?
Clem Oh. Sussex.
Matty I'm at Bristol.

Clem nods and turns to go

What did you read?
Clem Maths.
Matty Well, would you believe that. So am I.
Clem (*smiling*) I wish you luck.

Clem again turns to go. Mrs King closes the score decisively

Julia Young man, I really *need* another cup of coffee.

Act I, Scene 2

Clem Certainly, Madam. (*He goes to the counter for coffee*)
Hester That's a personable boy.
Henry I think Matty's noticed.
Julia Unusual to see a graduate working in the holidays. Most of them are layabouts ...
Hester Julia, you really are too didactic.
Julia You know how I stand on this. Educate them out of their class, and what happens? Waste of time and public money.
Hester No education is wasted ...
Julia Naturally, you wouldn't think so. But remember you always worked in high-grade girls' schools. Your own closed little world ...
Hester (*laughing*) I assure you the flesh *and* the devil crept in at times.
Mrs Stevens (*suddenly*) I only got three O-levels. I'm afraid I wasn't very good at exams.
Hester That's not unusual. I have had quite brilliant students who looked at their papers and went completely blank.
Julia I expect that's what happened to her ...

Clem brings the coffee

Thank you.
Henry And what do *you* do? Jobwise, I mean.
Clem I'm—in the transport business.
Henry Is that interesting?
Clem It has its moments.

Matty comes down to Clem and offers him a cigarette

No, thank you. Not just now ...
Matty Oh, come on. You're not that busy. Have a drink with us before we go. (*She goes up to the counter and takes a clean glass, which she brings back. There is a bottle of wine on the table. She fills their glasses*) Let's kill Henry's bottle.

Matty sits below the table. Clem stands between her and Henry. He lights his cigarette

Henry Your very good health.
Clem And to you.
Hester We come here most years, you know. It's the Choirs Festival at Hamlyn House ...
Mrs Brockett (*from the window*) His Lordship gives it over to us for the day. And tea in a big tent.
Hester Do you know about "Sing for Pleasure"?
Clem Sorry ...?
Julia It is a movement of choirs—amateur, of course. Now national with international connections. It's primarily a young organization but older people are welcome if they have the slightest voice ...
Mrs Brockett I got no voice at my age. But I help around and make the coffee. It gets me out, and it's a nice change from the telly.
Mrs Stevens (*suddenly*) It's just when everyone GETS UP ALL AT ONCE ... (*Her voice rises, she puts a hand to her eyes*)

Julia Oh, Lord—she's off ...
Hester Now, Phyllis, calm down ... } (*Speaking together*)

Mrs Brockett (*at the window*) You *would* bring her.

Hester Come into the cloakroom and wash your face—now come *along*—

Clem goes to the inner door and calls

Clem Lina ...!

Lina enters

Clem motions her behind the counter. She hesitates—he urges her on. This does not interrupt the dialogue at the table

Julia For goodness' sake—I'll take her. She needs a firm hand. Matty—got any tissues ...

Julia takes Mrs Stevens out through the inner door. Matty follows, collecting her big bag from the window in passing

Mrs Brockett I wouldn't mind a wash myself. (*She goes to the inner door and pauses, speaking across to the table*) Nerves. Weak-gutted, that's what I call it.

Mrs Brockett exits through the inner door. Clem follows

Hester What a pity. I thought we might get through without that.

Jubilee comes in quickly from the inner door and moves down to Joe. He makes an expressive gesture over his shoulder

Jubilee Flaming hell—I'm taking a turn outside ...

Joe nods

Jubilee exits through the main door

Hester Perhaps Brockett was right. We shouldn't have brought her.

Henry It's difficult for someone like Mrs Brockett or Julia to evaluate the effects of a nervous breakdown.

Hester (*quietly*) I know. But sometimes one must sit back and let things resolve——

Henry Yes, but we must *help* ...

Hester We *are* helping. We can't pad the poor little thing against ordinary everyday contacts. This singing is very good gentle therapy ...

Henry Julia's methods are more like shock treatment.

Hester (*laughing*) And the day Phyllis stands up to her, she's cured.

Henry (*slowly*) Hester—sooner or later we have to do something about Julia.

Hester Not yet. It may all settle down. Julia means very well and she knows her subject. She gets too involved and then she forgets she's dealing with people.

Act I, Scene 2

Henry Don't you think we should—just delicately—speak to her?
Hester No, I don't. As I said, it may settle down. If it doesn't, then Julia will have to sort it out by herself.
Henry If I didn't know you so well, I'd say you had no compassion.
Hester (*smiling*) Dear Henry, you have too much. That's why you get involved.
Henry Involvement is my job. Or should be.
Hester It's a delicate balance. Too little is not enough. Too much and one gets hurt.
Henry One is constantly hurt. One simply cannot get through—I'm beginning to wonder if I did right to enter the Church ...
Hester May I say something, Henry?
Henry My dear Hester, please do.
Hester You want to give so much all at once. Take it gently. You can't rush people on a spiritual issue.
Henry I think ...
Hester (*laughing*) I think you would have made a wonderful medieval monk. Dedicated, fanatical—forcing every man upon his own salvation ...
Henry What's wrong with that?
Hester You would have argued with your superiors and ended at the stake.
Henry And so failed.
Hester Failed? How?
Henry Because it would have been a political, not a spiritual, execution.
Hester Yes, I do see. To die for someone's ambitions and not for one's personal beliefs. Quite horrid—do you think that nice little girl would bring us another cup of coffee?
Henry I'll get it. (*He goes to the counter, smiling at Joe as he passes. To Lina*) Could I have another cup of coffee, please?
Lina Sure, Mr Cole. I bring it over.
Henry That's all right. I'll wait.
Lina No, no, Mr Cole. You sit down. I bring it.
Henry If you say so. (*He turns back, speaking to Joe as he goes*) Nice day.
Joe Sure.

Henry sits down above the table and talks to Hester. Lina pours coffee from the Cona and takes it over to them

Hester Thank you.
Henry Haven't had much time to talk to you today, Lina. How are you?
Lina Very well, Mr Cole, thank you, sir.
Henry Busy?
Lina Not so much now. With the new motorway comin' we're just cut off the main road ...
Henry Yes, I do see that ...

Joe reaches for the matches at the top end of the counter, pauses, glancing over. Lina bends down and pretends to brush some crumbs from the table

Lina (*in a very low voice*) Mr Cole ...

Henry Yes, Lina. (*Suddenly puzzled*) What is it?
Lina (*whispering*) Mr Cole, I got to tell you . . .

Joe stands up. Her voice cuts across

Joe Waitress . . .!

Lina straightens up

May I have a packet of crisps?
Lina You like to take them from shelf?

Joe moves to the middle of the room, looking at Lina

Joe Cheese and onion—please.

Lina goes to the counter. Joe brings cigarettes from her pocket and offers the packet to Henry

Henry (*smiling*) I don't, thanks.
Joe (*lightly*) Lucky old you.

Lina comes down and gives Joe a packet of crisps

Thanks. Settle it all up when we go.

Lina goes back behind the counter. She sits on the stool, moving it close back against the shelves. Joe offers the cigarettes to Hester

Hester I don't either. Unfortunately.
Joe Unfortunately? (*She lights a cigarette*)
Hester I enjoyed tobacco. I found it relaxing and conducive to thought. Then I had bronchitis and it became a straight choice. Give up smoking or choke to death.
Joe Nasty.
Hester Yes. Even five years later there are moments of tension when I automatically reach for a cigarette. Do you live round here?
Joe Not far.
Hester Do you know the Marshalls?
Joe Not intimately.
Hester (*laughing*) I expect you thought we were a little mad just now. First the singing and then our poor friend—she's just getting over a nervous breakdown . . .
Joe Hard luck.
Hester Yes, but it is a little disconcerting when someone loses control in public. I hope it didn't disturb you?
Joe Disturb? (*She laughs, shortly*) No. It didn't disturb me in the least.

Jubilee enters from outside and goes to the stool at the upstage end of the counter

Joe Excuse me. (*She goes to Jubilee, offers him a cigarette and sits on the downstage stool*)
Hester Now I wonder what's wrong there?
Henry Wrong? Nothing. She just isn't very talkative.

Act I, Scene 2

Hester No. I spent my life—my working life—among young people. Something has gone deep. Very deep, I hope ...
Henry Hope what?
Hester I hope whatever it is, it isn't too late. (*She laughs*) I've had too much of your wine. How much time have we got?

They both look at their watches

Henry We're all right for ten minutes or so. I wonder how soon they'll be ready in there?
Hester (*getting up*) I'll go and see.
Henry Right. I'm just going outside ...

Hester goes out by the inner door, Henry by the main door

Joe turns on Lina

Joe I warned you, didn't I! Just you try anything like that again. You hear?
Jubilee What she do?
Joe Tried to warn the parson. (*To Lina*) You make one more step out of line—just one, mind—and I swear I'll crack you from here to Easter. Right?

Lina does not answer

Right?

Lina nods sullenly

Jubilee I said it was too dicey. We should have got off——
Joe They'll be away in a minute or two. That idiot creature with the flim-flams is holding things up.
Jubilee Cor—what a crowd. Makes me glad.
Joe Glad what?
Jubilee Glad I'm on the other side to them. Where's Clem?
Joe (*laughing*) Counting the silver in the kitchen. (*Quickly*) Watch it ...

Hester enters from the inner door, followed by Mrs Brockett. They go to the table and collect their handbags, etc. Mrs Brockett puts her cardigan over her shoulders. Matty comes in and goes to the windowseat to collect her book and spectacles

Hester With any luck she'll be all right now. Did Mrs King give her anything?
Mrs Brockett She'd got her own tablets—great red things. You're not expecting her to *sing*?
Hester We'll see when we get there. It may do her good.
Mrs Brockett Won't do much good to them who got to listen. Let's just hope she stands there with her mouth shut.

Julia and Mrs Stevens enter from the inner door and go to the table

Julia All ready? Where's Henry?

Hester Just gone to the toilet. No immediate hurry—we may as well sit down.

Hester, Mrs Brockett and Mrs Stevens sit at the table. Julia remains standing above it

Julia It's another thirty miles. And I did want a run through of the united choirs at the end . . .
Hester Don't worry, Julia . . .
Julia I *have* been selected as guest conductor—and apart from all this, we really should take a look at our "Merry Month of May".
Mrs Stevens (*suddenly, plaintively*) I don't like that one . . .
Julia That's all right. You're not in it.
Mrs Stevens Those repeating bits are very difficult. I get breathless on the top notes . . .
Julia I've told you over and over again about breath control. Sometimes I don't think you *listen* . . .
Hester (*gently*) You do very well. And you come over beautifully in "Hark, hark the lark".
Mrs Stevens (*complacently*) Yes, I do, don't I? (*Abruptly*) Who's going to drive this time?
Julia If Hester doesn't mind, I am.
Mrs Stevens Then may I sit in the back, please. I feel safer.

Julia turns angrily

Hester (*quickly*) Of course you may. I'll sit with you.
Matty (*at the window*) Here's Henry.

Henry enters from outside

Julia Ah, there you are, Henry. We really should be going.
Henry Plenty of time. Just all sit a moment while I settle the bill. (*Taking out his wallet*) What do we owe you, Lina?

Lina takes a small pad from under the counter and goes towards the table

Hester Let me do this, Henry . . .
Henry Certainly not.

Lina makes out the bill

Julia You can make it a legitimate tax deduction.
Henry You bet. Well, what does it come to?
Lina That'll be six pounds forty-two pence, Mr Cole, sir. You brought your own wine.

Clem enters from inside and stands above the counter. Henry counts notes on the table

Henry . . . Four, five, six. That's very reasonable, you know. (*He finds change in his trouser pocket*) Ten, twenty, thirty, forty and a two. All right?

Act I, Scene 2

Lina Thank you, sir.

Henry takes two notes from his wallet. He gives one to Lina

Henry And that's for you. Thank you for your help.
Lina Thank you, sir. Thank you indeed.

Henry goes to Clem and gives him the other note

Henry And many thanks to you. You've given us a really good lunch and a pleasant stay.
Clem Thank *you*, sir. It's been a pleasure.

Clem pockets the note. Henry moves back, putting away his wallet

Lina Your bill, Mr Cole, sir. I put receipt for tax. Six pounds, forty-two . . .

Lina tears off the slip and gives it to him. She goes back to the counter, putting the pad at the lower end. Henry glances at the bill. For a split second, he stiffens. Joe suddenly looks down at the pad. Henry puts the bill in his pocket. He goes and opens the main door

Henry (*cheerfully*) Right, everyone. We go.

Joe stands up

Joe (*quietly*) All right, Henry.

They all turn. She has her gun in her hand. Clem and Jubilee bring out their guns. Mrs Stevens gives a little gasp and puts her hand over her mouth

Henry What does this . . .
Joe Shut the door, Henry.
Henry I . . .
Joe Shut the door.

Henry shuts the door

Bolt it.

Henry bolts the door

You—with the car keys. Put them on the table.

Hester puts the keys on the table

Jube . . .

Jubilee goes to the table and puts the car keys in his pocket

Now move your flock, Henry. Back along that wall.

Henry indicates to the others. They line up along the wall behind the table

And now the bill, Henry. Come on. I saw you put it in your pocket.

Henry hesitates

(*Gently*) The *bill*, Henry.

Henry takes the bill from his pocket

How much was it? Six pounds forty-two?
Henry Yes.
Joe Is that what it says?
Henry Yes.
Joe Henry, I'm ashamed of you. You're a disgrace to your Church. Shall I tell you what it says? (*She puts her gun on the counter and holds out the billpad. There are a couple of blank pages on top. She flips them over. A thin blue slip flutters out. Reading*) "Bad men from prison. Get police..." (*She turns on Lina*) Stupid damned wog—you forgot the carbon!

Joe swings up her arm for the vicious backhand blow. Before it descends, Lina falls to her knees, arms over her head

Clem (*shouting*) JOE...!

CURTAIN

ACT II

The same. One hour later

The party are back in their old places, except that Matty now sits below the table. Jubilee is on the windowseat, his gun on his knee

As the CURTAIN *rises, Lina enters from inside carrying a tray with cutlery and plates of food. Joe follows with a dish of vegetables*

Joe Make room, please. We want three places.

Lina sets the table. Henry moves above the counter. Hester follows and sits on the upstage stool. Julia moves to the downstage stool. Matty and Mrs Brockett take Mrs King to the windowseat and stand waiting pointedly for Jubilee to get up. He looks up, rises and goes down and round to the lower end of the table. Joe sits behind the table, Clem moves in beside her. Lina goes back with the tray behind the counter. Joe, Clem and Jubilee eat and talk among themselves

Lina (*quietly*) I'm sorry, Mr Cole, sir.
Henry Sorry, Lina? Why?
Lina I tried be too clever. If I hadn't done that bill you'd have gone and known nuthin' about it.
Hester No—you were perfectly right.
Julia I should think so indeed. These people can't be allowed to get away with it . . .
Henry (*ruefully*) They have for the moment. There isn't much we can do . . .
Hester I can't believe they'd actually use those guns.
Julia Of course they would. One reads about it in the papers every day.
Hester Has it occurred to you that we shall probably end up front-page news ourselves?
Joe (*calling*) Three Cokes over here, please.

Lina takes over three cans

Julia If they interview me, I shall make it extremely clear where I stand on this question of maximum security prisons. Not to say violence *in toto*.

Lina returns to the stool behind the counter

Henry (*wryly*) And demand they bring back hanging.
Julia Certainly. The way the world is going, it will eventually become an economic necessity.
Hester (*gently*) Oh, Julia, dear—you do lay down the law . . .
Julia As a practising magistrate, Hester, I not only know more about the law than you do, but about the people who continually break it. Look at that lot over there. Not a scrap of conscience between them.

Hester The older man is obviously an habitual. I should like to know how the two young ones came to this.
Julia Quite simple. The boy's weak. The girl's bad.
Henry You allow them no chance...?
Julia The boy's apparently a graduate. A lot of the taxpayers' money has gone towards giving him a chance. What's he done with it...

Mrs Brockett comes to the counter with her handbag

Mrs Brockett (*To Lina*) Can we have a cup of coffee, dearie? (*To Hester*) We think we'd better give her her tablets again.
Hester I think she's taking it very well.
Mrs Brockett Do we have to take it at all? I mean—six of us—there must be *something* we can do.
Henry We need to know what they're going to do first. They won't stay here indefinitely. And they certainly can't take us with them.

Lina puts a cup of coffee on the counter. Mrs Brockett takes some coins from her bag

Mrs Brockett Thanks, dearie. That's right, isn't it?
Lina You don't give money now...
Mrs Brockett Listen to me, young lady. I've paid my way since I left school at fourteen, and that lot over there's not going to alter my principles now. (*She slaps down the coins and takes the coffee to Mrs Stevens*)

Lina puts the coins in the till

Joe (*calling*) Another cup over here, Lina.

Lina pours a cup

Hester (*quietly, to Lina*) Give that to me.

Hester takes the coffee to Joe. Lina sits on the stool behind the counter, moving it back against the shelves

Joe That's very civil of you—(*mockingly*)—Ma'am. (*To Jubilee*) Shows the right spirit, don't you think? Democratic.

Jubilee nods and belches

You must excuse him—Ma'am. He's not been living among polite society lately. Have you, Jube?
Jubilee (*softly*) Lay off, will you!

Jubilee goes behind the counter, takes a packet of cigarettes, and goes out through the inner door: he is seen passing across the window at the back

Joe Used to smooth people, aren't you? Ran a girls' school or something?
Hester Yes.
Joe Headmistress, of course.
Hester (*quietly*) For fifteen years I was Principal of Hexworth...
Clem Hexworth...

Act II

Joe What's so special?
Clem One of the most famous girls' schools in the country. On a par with Roedean.
Joe I see. Nice good little girls with nice good little manners. Never did a bad thing—or said a bad word ...
Hester (*quietly*) It was a school. Not a convent.
Joe (*lighting a cigarette*) And in fifteen years, you never got stuck with a baddie?
Hester With a cross-section of humanity, there can be difficulties. I remember one girl who came from a grammar school—and incidentally from a far from good background ...
Joe I bet she hated you all.
Hester At that time, she hated the world.
Joe So what did you do? Beat her to death? Or just—freeze—her out?
Hester Neither. She went on to Oxford, read science, is now teaching, and recently published a very well-researched paper on horology.
Joe Horo ...?
Clem Clocks.
Joe Clocks! (*Laughing*) Lord save us—clocks. What a waste of time.

Clem laughs

So what's the joke?
Clem Clocks. Time. Waste of time ...
Joe (*disgustedly*) Oh, brilliant!
Julia If you've finished being social, Hester, you might ask them what they propose to do about us.
Hester I was coming to that. (*To Joe*) Have you any objection? To telling us?
Joe Not really. (*She gets up and stretches*)
Julia Well, then?
Joe We'll think about you.
Clem Does it matter? Why not——
Joe Let them sweat it out ... (*She pauses*)

A car engine is heard running

What the hell ... (*She goes to the window and looks off, her gun suddenly in her hand*) It's Jubilee—no—(*to the three on the windowseat*)—stay where you are.
Clem (*getting up*) What's he doing?
Joe All right. He's putting the car in the barn. Good thinking. (*Laughing*) He's been dying to get his hands on it. Massive great thing. Whose is it?
Hester Mine.

Hester sits above the table. Matty sits beside her

Joe Yours? And why should you have a car like that?
Hester (*quietly*) I worked for it.
Joe Lucky old you.

Joe goes to the upstage stool. Henry gets up for her. She sits down, gun on knee

Thanks, Henry. They taught you pretty manners.
Matty (*suddenly*) You can't keep us here indefinitely, you know.
Joe Who says so?
Matty We're not just out for a casual drive. We're expected by three o'clock. We're part of a festival.
Joe I should think they'd be more festive without you.
Matty You don't understand. Mrs King is to conduct the choir. My aunt accompanies them. If we don't turn up they'll try to find us . . .
Joe How?
Matty They know we were stopping here for lunch. They'll probably telephone.
Joe Too bad they won't get a reply.
Julia Then they'll think we've met with an accident, and probably alert the police.
Clem That's a point, Joe . . .
Joe Shut up. (*She looks at the party*) Get this clear. We're staying here till dark. We shall then lock you in the storeroom. It's ventilated. There's food and drink. The owners will be back on Monday. It'll no doubt be a bit of a shock but no-one's going to die of it.
Matty Look—would you let us go if we gave our word not to say anything . . .
Julia That we would not. Are you out of your mind?
Mrs Stevens (*piping up*) I don't think we should—not say anything, I mean . . .
Mrs Brockett (*suddenly*) Well, I wish somebody would make their minds up. I can see she means what she says, right enough, and I'm not sitting here for forty-eight hours doing nothing. (*She gets up and faces Joe*) Now, my girl—just you get one of your boy-friends out to that car and fetch my knitting.

Joe looks at her. She laughs

Joe No way, grandma. No way.

Mrs Stevens gets up abruptly

Mrs Stevens I'll go. It's on the back seat . . . (*She starts for the main door*)

Clem is there first, with his back to the door

Julia Phyllis . . . !
Joe Back to your own seat, sweetie. Fast.
Mrs Stevens (*plaintively*) What *is* the fuss about? You'll all be watching me with those guns, won't you? So I've got to come back, haven't I?
Julia (*to Henry*) Those must be pretty powerful pills.
Joe Get right back over there.
Mrs Stevens I'm not used to this, really I'm not. Not used to it at all. (*Her voice falters. She goes to the windowseat and blows her nose*)

Mrs Brockett joins them

Act II

Clem Let her have it, Joe. Can't do any harm. I'll get it. Right?
Joe Suit yourself.

Joe sits down again on the upstage stool. She makes a gesture to Henry and Julia who go and sit at the table with Hester. Clem unbolts the door and calls

Clem Jube . . . !
Jubilee (*some little way off*) Hullo?
Clem Back seat of car. There's . . . (*To Mrs Brockett*) What's it like?
Mrs Brockett Brown paper carrier-bag. Says Biggs's Stores.
Clem (*calling*) Brown paper grocer's bag.
Jubilee (*off*) Will do.

Clem closes the door and bolts it. He sits down above the table

Mrs Brockett Thank you.

There is a pause. Matty speaks suddenly

Matty It's odd. We ought to feel scared. And I don't. Only angry. Very angry.
Hester That's normal, darling. Your adrenalin's working.
Mrs Stevens I'm not scared. At least—only when I think about it.
Mrs Brockett Then stop thinking, dear.
Julia That shouldn't be difficult.

Jubilee passes the window from the main door, then enters from the inner door. He carries a brown paper carrier printed in large letters "BIGGS' BACON". It has knitting and a magazine sticking out

Jubilee Crissake—what a car. Handles like a dream——

Jubilee goes to Joe, putting the bag at the end of the counter. Mrs Brockett gets it, goes back to her seat and starts knitting

—pity we can't take off in it.
Joe Might just as well knock off a police car.
Jubilee I know. I know. But one day I'm going to get a car like that. And mightn't be so long at that, eh? (*He puts his arm round her and gives her a squeeze*)
Joe (*quietly*) I said watch that.

Another glance passes between them. Jubilee sits on the upstage stool. Joe looks at her watch and yawns. She gets up

I'm going to have a wash and a nap in there. You two take over. And you lot—no tricks, mind.

Joe goes to the inner door. Julia gets up

Julia I'll come with you. I take it we'll only be allowed to go under armed guard.
Joe That's it. (*She gestures to Julia to go past her*) And don't take too long, either.

Julia goes out through the inner door. Joe follows

Jubilee yawns. He gets up and goes to the stool by the main door, takes a handkerchief and his gun from his pocket and cleans the gun carefully

Joe puts her head round the inner door

Joe Clem . . .
Clem Yes?
Joe Call me in about half an hour.
Clem Sure.

Joe withdraws her head

Matty Is she really the boss?
Clem She knows what she's doing. Joe's all right.
Matty Is she your girl-friend?
Clem Yes.
Matty Where did you meet her?
Hester (*gently*) You ask too many questions, darling. Personal ones.
Matty I just wondered. (*To Clem*) Not at University?
Clem No.
Matty What did you get? Degree, I mean.
Clem (*laughing shortly*) Your aunt's right. You do ask too many questions.
Matty I'm sorry. I was only interested . . .
Clem I got a first. Think of that, now. Maths. First-class honours.
Henry That was encouraging . . .
Clem Don't be so patronizing. It was bloody good.
Henry I beg your pardon. I didn't mean . . .
Clem Yes, you did. And you're coming up to the next bit, aren't you?
Henry Next . . . ?
Clem The bit about how did I come to this and what a waste of a good brain. I've heard it all before, Henry. From the magistrates. From the judge.
Hester (*gently*) Could they perhaps be right?
Clem I'm not arguing. One doesn't argue with people who don't know the facts.
Hester What facts?
Clem The facts up here. (*He touches his forehead*) The facts that make people do what they do.
Henry I think you're . . .
Clem (*not listening*) That woman—that magistrate. She sits up on the bench with two others. They're told a few things in about three minutes. They ask footling questions for another three minutes. Then they make a decision. About something which could have been building up for years.
Henry How long has it built up with you?
Clem It doesn't matter.
Hester It should matter. It's your life.

Act II

Clem You're so right, lady. That's exactly what it is. My life and no-one else's.

Matty I thought you were sharing it with Joe.

Clem looks at her for a second

Clem (*quietly*) Auntie, you must teach your niece to keep her little claws hidden.
Matty But you...
Hester (*quietly*) Leave it alone, Matty.
Matty I...
Hester Just leave it alone.
Clem (*laughing*) Poor little kitty. She didn't mean anything. Here... (*He offers Matty a cigarette*) Let her be happy while she can. The cold hard world is waiting outside...

The telephone rings. Instantly Lina, leaning against the wall beside it, snatches it up. The moment is completely unguarded, Jubilee cleaning his gun, Clem offering Matty a cigarette

Lina (*on the telephone*) Prospect Café—yes, they're here. (*Calling*) Mis' King...

Jubilee is behind her almost before she finishes speaking, holding her against him, his hand over her mouth. Clem is up, gun ready

Joe rushes in through the inner door—Julia stands in the doorway

Jubilee grabs the telephone to replace it

Joe No—wait!

Joe grabs Matty and pulls her against her, facing outwards, the gun in her ribs

(*To Julia*) You—answer it. Your car's broken down—you're coming later. Any funny business—she gets it! Move!

Julia hesitates. Jubilee pushes Lina in front of him through the downstage opening of the counter and pins her against the wall downstage. Julia goes behind the counter and takes the telephone

(*Warningly*) Careful...!
Julia (*on the telephone*) Julia Saunders-King. Who is that?... Oh, Mary, yes.... Yes, most unfortunate—we've not had time to get on to you. The car's broken down.... Yes, a garage just near.... We don't quite know. It may not be very much.... No, no. I think it best to wait.... No—nothing to worry about. We'll be there as soon as we can. Give our apologies to his Lordship.... Thank you. (*She starts to replace the telephone, then pauses*) Oh, Mary—just in case we're not there by three—better let me speak to Mrs Prescott.... Yes, his lordship will know....
Joe What're you up to? Hang up...
Julia (*to Joe*) You want things to sound normal, don't you? Since we're

not going to be there, I have to make alternative arrangements for my singers.

Joe Put that phone down—you've been cut off . . .

Julia Then I shall be expected to ring back. They're not fools, you know——

Joe Hang up!

Clem (*quickly*) She's right, Joe . . .

Joe I said hang——

Julia (*on the telephone*) Hullo—Sybil? . . . Good. Now listen. We may be delayed. You'll have to conduct. . . . Yes. Yes, I know you will. Take them briskly through "Shepherds and Neighbours"—and try to control Emily Parsons on the trills. . . . (*Laughing*) I know, I know. Now, Sybil—just one thing. For the second piece I want you to do the *Judas Maccabaeus*. . . . Yes, that's right. It's aria forty-five. Forty-five. The first line is vital—they must get that right. If you're not sure, ask his Lordship—he's sure to have a score of his own. . . .

Joe (*hissing*) Cut it out!

Julia (*on the telephone*) I must go, Sybil. Someone is calling—some petrol-boy. . . . Yes—just as soon as we can. Best of luck. Good-bye. (*She replaces the receiver*)

Joe gestures towards the table

Joe Over there. Move!

Julia goes and sits at the downstage end of the table. Joe thrusts Matty away. Clem catches her, sitting her above the table. Hester puts an arm round her

Now—let's have the little wog. Over here, Jube.

Clem (*quickly*) Joe . . .

Joe You keep your eyes on that lot.

Jubilee brings Lina up to face Joe

(*To Lina, quietly*) Proper little trier, aren't you? Must be all that black blood. (*She puts the gun muzzle under Lina's chin and tilts her head up*) I ought to beat you within an inch of your life . . .

Henry No!
Julia Don't you . . . } (*Speaking together*)

Joe (*without turning*) Quiet! (*To Lina*) Don't worry. I wouldn't soil my hands. But we must make sure you don't get up to any more little tricks. Jube—lock her in the storeroom.

Joe takes the keys from her pocket and gives them to Jubilee

Jubilee takes Lina out by the inner door

Joe moves behind the counter, putting the gun close to hand on the top

Julia Brutality . . .

Joe Survival. (*She pours a cup of coffee, and sits on the stool behind the counter*)

Hester (*gently*) Does it really give you pleasure to be cruel?

Act II

Joe She can move around. She has air—and food.
Hester She's scared and she's alone . . .
Joe Not for long. You'll all be joining her in an hour or two.
Henry Let me go in with her.
Joe (*laughing*) You'd like that, Henry, wouldn't you? Shut in there with the little wog. Or are you celibate? Have to go without for the glory of the Lord?
Julia You're disgusting . . .
Joe Nothing disgusting about it. Coloureds are people same as anyone else. And she's not bad as they go. Big dark eyes, and a nice pair in the right place. Eh, Henry?
Julia Ignore her.
Joe *Are* you married, Henry? Well, come on. It's a fair question.
Henry No.
Joe And you, ma'am? Career woman?
Hester (*quietly*) A little while ago you said we talked too much. Aren't you doing rather a lot yourself?
Joe We're stuck with you till dark. Just now, I need amusing. So go on. Amuse me.
Julia (*getting up*) Personally, I have no intention of doing anything of the kind. I see people like you often enough in the courts. And you certainly don't amuse *me*. (*She goes to the windowseat and sits*)
Joe (*under her breath*) Cow. (*To the others*) So go on. Talk.
Matty What about?
Joe What makes you tick.
Matty Our hearts, our lungs, our brains. Exactly like you.
Joe I don't mean that—and you know it. So don't get clever with me.
Matty I wouldn't presume . . .
Hester (*very quietly*) Darling, don't provoke her.
Joe And don't whisper among yourselves. It's not good manners.
Hester Then here's another fair question. How do you define good manners?
Joe (*laughing*) You think I can't?

Jubilee returns. He goes across to Clem and leans against the wall beside him. They talk together

Joe moves down from the counter and stands in the middle of the room

Well—ma'am. Suppose I wanted something from you. That watch, say—looks nice and small and expensive. Jubilee there, he'd hold you with one hand and take it with the other—(*she snaps her fingers*)—pff—so. That's bad manners.
Hester And you . . . ?
Joe I'd *ask* you. Ever so politely. To take it off and hand it over. When you did, I'd say thank you. That's good manners.
Hester And if one didn't just take off the watch and hand it over?
Joe (*laughing*) Why, then I'd have to whistle up Jubilee.
Matty Would you take the watch because you wanted it? Or on the broad general principle that it belonged to someone else?

Joe Because it belonged to people like you. The smoothies. With the estates, the cars and the inherited money...
Hester We don't quite come under that heading...
Joe You keep talking about his Lordship. You're in that circle.
Hester Why are you so opposed to inherited money?
Joe It comes without working for it.
Hester No. Somewhere along the line, back a few generations, perhaps—someone worked for it. Let me put it to you like this. If you worked hard and made a great deal of money...
Joe (*laughing*) That'd be the day.
Hester When you died the Government would take a great amount in tax. Would you not want to leave the rest to your children?
Joe Of course.
Hester Would they not then be living on inherited money?
Joe (*laughing*) Ah—you just said I'd have earned it in the first place. You're not talking much, Henry. Cat got your tongue?
Henry (*half to himself*) "Sell all that thou hast and give it to the poor."
Joe Sounds very good advice to me.
Matty Someone else gave good advice, too. A man called Abraham Lincoln.
Joe (*yawning*) So what did Abe say, then?
Matty "You do not help the poor by destroying the rich."
Joe Henry's character had more sense. That was a right guy. Who is he?
Henry Jesus Christ.

A slight pause. Joe laughs

Joe I might have known. Well, you clever lot, I've got one for you. "That which you want—take it."
Matty And pay for it.
Joe Come again?
Matty It's a Spanish proverb. "Take what you want, said God. Take it—and pay for it." (*Quietly*) If you must quote, quote correctly.

Matty and Joe look at each other. Joe's face changes

Joe You make me *sick*. (*She turns away*)
Henry Could we ask you—please—to let that girl out?

Joe swings round

Joe Shut up! All of you. Any more arguments and the lot of you go in there. Now.
Matty Perhaps in the circumstances we'd prefer it.
Hester *Matty...!*
Joe You'll go when I say so and not before. That girl's going to be taught a lesson. She can have a taste of what solitary's like. (*She moves to the counter*) Clem...

Clem follows Joe to the counter. She sits on the stool behind, he sits on the upstage stool. They talk. Jubilee yawns and stretches. He sees the carrier-bag on the floor and pulls out the magazine

Act II

Mrs Brockett (*ironically*) Help yourself, do. Though I shouldn't hardly think it's your sort of reading.
Jubilee *Woman Today*. (*He grins*) Are they any different from yesterday? (*He opens out the magazine and laughs*) Not by this they're not. Oh, well—it might be interesting. (*He sits on the stool by the main door and reads*)

Julia gets up and goes to the chair below the table

Mrs Stevens (*suddenly*) Emily Parsons never *will* get those trills right.
Julia Well, we shall just have to hope she does.
Mrs Stevens I do them rather well.
Julia Yes, dear. When you're in tune.
Mrs Stevens What you said—on the phone—about that Judas thing—I don't . . .
Julia You were away when we rehearsed it. Anyhow, it's not in your range.
Mrs Stevens I'm high soprano. My range is very good. I just have to *concentrate* . . .
Mrs Brockett If you don't concentrate on that pattern, my grandson won't get this pullover to be buried in. Now—(*indicating with her needle*)—what's after repeat from star . . . ?
Mrs Stevens Three purl, three plain, slip two, knit two together . . . (*She looks at the piece of knitting*) I don't like the colour very much.
Mrs Brockett Right now, all I'm concerned about is the *shape*.
Mrs Stevens I don't like that very much, either.
Matty I wonder Mrs Brockett doesn't crown her.
Julia Brockett has worked for me for over twenty years. If that hasn't taught her patience, nothing ever will.
Matty She isn't scared, either.
Mrs Brockett (*knitting busily*) What've I got to be scared about? I've got my health and strength and a clear conscience. (*Grimly*) And thirty years of a hard marriage to toughen me up as well.
Matty Why, Brockie—I thought you had a happy married life?
Mrs Brockett Not me. (*Shaking her head*) No. Never thought much to Brockett after the first six months.
Matty But you had ten children . . .
Mrs Brockett What's that got to do with it? (*She draws out a needle, scratches her head with it and goes on knitting*)

Matty giggles

Hester (*laughing*) Perhaps that was part of the toughening-up process.
Matty It's a salutary thought—what would her life have been if her generation had had the pill?
Julia She has six sons and two daughters living—all healthy—all semi-articulate—and all doing extremely well.
Henry Don't I know it! Tom Brockett services my old Mini. He runs a Rover Two Thousand himself. Brand new.
Matty (*suddenly, softly*) Oh, my God . . .

Matty half rises. Hester pulls her down again

Hester (*gently*) All right, darling. Sit quietly. You're still a bit shocked.
Matty No—I'm sorry—I'm all right. Really I am. But we're—we're just *sitting* here—doing nothing—talking trivialities . . .
Henry We just have to be patient. A few hours and they'll be gone.
Matty And we'll be shut up for a day and two nights . . .
Hester It's not eternity. And we'll all be together.
Henry I suppose nothing will persuade her to let Lina out . . .
Matty You won't persuade her to do anything. She's evil. Completely evil . . .
Hester Matty, dear . . .
Matty Have you noticed—she dominates everyone—and she never—never—raises her voice. And I'll tell you something else. When she held me—up there—with that gun in my ribs—her hand didn't shake. And—and——
Julia Don't, Matty . . .
Matty —I was pressed up against her. I could feel her heart . . .
Henry Matty . . .
Matty (*quietly*) It was as steady as a ticking clock. It never missed a beat. (*She pauses, looking at them*) I think if she—had shot me—it would never have missed a beat. She's completely evil. I don't think I've ever—hated anyone so much.
Henry (*with sudden authority*) Matty!
Matty Yes, Henry?
Henry I beg you not to hate her. If you do, then she has transferred some of her evil to you.
Matty You have to say that. It's your job . . .
Henry But I understand, Matty. She terrifies me, too.
Julia Nonsense, Henry. I do not for one moment believe she would use that gun.
Henry Then are you prepared to go and take it from her?
Julia Are *you*?
Henry No. But not from fear of being wounded—or even killed.
Julia What then?
Henry I can't look at her—let alone speak to her. She makes me feel helpless—and inadequate. (*To Hester*) And you talked about a burning zeal—and martyrdom.
Hester (*quietly*) Deliver us from the restless evil.
Henry The . . .?
Hester Something I learned to recognize in young people. A kind of restlessness—when the evil which is in all of us can easily take over. It is then one's job—one's privilege rather, to try and help them fight it.
Matty How?
Hester Work. Discipline. Above all, understanding. (*Gently*) Things you've had all your life, Matty. I wonder if that girl has known any of them.
Julia Really—you make the creature sound powerful and important. Get your values right. She's a petty little criminal who should be behind bars . . .
Henry She's a human being, created by God.
Julia One of His less worthy efforts.

Act II

Henry Who desperately needs our help and compassion.
Matty No. It is *not* right. We make excuses for these people. The ordinary honest ones often suffer—even die—rather than do wrong. No-one is concerned for them. But let one old lag in prison start whining he misses his wife—and the do-gooders weep all over him.
Julia (*drily*) If that's what they taught you at Bristol, I congratulate your tutors.
Jubilee (*suddenly*) Cor . . . (*He turns a page of the magazine*)

The group at the table continue arguing inaudibly

Mrs Stevens What made him do that?
Mrs Brockett I think he's got to "Passion in the Peaks".
Mrs Stevens (*puzzled*) What peaks?
Mrs Brockett Mountain peaks. "Passion in the Peaks". It's the *serial*.
Mrs Stevens Oh. (*Considering*) I shouldn't think it would be very comfortable. I mean—all those *rocks* . . .
Mrs Brockett You just keep your mind on this decreasing . . .
Julia . . . and in the end it all comes down to a simple principle of *right* and *wrong*.
Henry No, no. If you——

Hester picks up the score

Hester Where we're really going wrong, is on this project for next season. I really don't think we can tackle "Unto us a Child is Born"—even with this arrangement for all female voices.
Julia You're changing the subject, Hester. And if I may say so, not very subtly.
Hester Quite right. But this must be discussed before the next Committee Meeting. So why not now? At least we have the time.
Mrs Stevens (*suddenly*) Perhaps they had a little *hut*.
Julia What *is* she talking about?
Mrs Stevens In the mountains. A little hut.
Julia What about it?
Mrs Stevens For the passion. I mean—it *would* be warmer in a little hut, wouldn't it?
Julia Have you gone . . . ?
Mrs Brockett It's all right—she's just got her wires crossed. Here—hold this, dear. I want to measure it. (*She gives Mrs Stevens the end of the knitting, takes a tape from her carrier-bag and measures*)
Julia I was about to say I am not necessarily considering an all-woman version. I propose trying to bring in some of the men.
Matty You'll never do it. They'll all turn brick red and rush for the nearest pub . . .

The discussion becomes inaudible

Joe Look at them. I hate their guts.
Clem Oh, they're harmless.
Joe Smug, that's what they are. For all they know we could turn trigger-happy and shoot them down in cold blood.

Clem They don't believe that.
Joe That's what I mean. Think they're something apart. (*Scornfully*) Choirs, festivals, ten kids—and that petted little virgin. They don't know they're alive.
Clem (*laughing*) And you don't know she's a virgin.
Joe I'd take a sizeable bet on it. And I'd bet on something else, too. She's not only a virgin. She's frigid.
Clem She's an intellectual.
Joe Gawd help her. She's another one who's never going to live.
Jubilee (*suddenly*) Crissake . . . !

Everyone stops talking. They all look at Jubilee

Listen to this. There's this woman here—calls herself Mrs Merryweather—Merryweather, what a mouthful—it seems these girls write letters to her—ask her things . . .
Clem Yes, Jube. It's known as the "so-help-me" page.
Jubilee I don't believe it. They must be out of their tiny minds. Listen. "Dear Mrs Merryweather—my boy-friend says he is not satisfied with heavy petting." (*He looks up*) Heavy petting—what's that for crissake? (*Reading again*) "He says we should go the whole way. But I told him I feel this is not right until we are married. Now he says I am not passionate. What should I do?" (*He looks up*) Do? I know what the boy-friend ought to do. He ought to . . .
Mrs Brockett (*knitting busily*) Buy a little hut.
Jubilee (*blankly*) What?
Mrs Brockett Never mind. What does Mrs Merryweather say?
Jubilee Eh?
Mrs Brockett If you read on, you'll see a reply.

Jubilee looks at the magazine

Jubilee Mm, mm mm—oh, yeah. Here. She says "Dear Worried . . ." what's she worried about—she's got a feller, hasn't she? "Dear Worried. Stand on your principles . . ."—(*laughing*)—so long as she doesn't stand on his—"if you give way to him, you will deeply regret it. Save yourself for the marriage night . . ." (*He throws down the magazine*) I never read such crap in all my life. (*He jerks his head at Mrs Brockett*) And what's she reading that stuff for at her age? Bit past heavy petting, isn't she?
Mrs Brockett (*to Jubilee*) Stand up, will you?
Jubilee Eh?

Mrs Brockett gets up

Mrs Brockett Stand up a moment while I measure this. You're about the same size as my grandson. He's a big lad for his age. (*She shakes out the pullover*)
Jubilee Flaming hell I will!
Mrs Brockett Hold up your arms . . .
Clem (*laughing*) Go on, Jube. Why not?
Jubilee What does she think I am? Flaming male model?

Act II

Mrs Brockett You might have done worse. Probably a fine-looking chap in your time.
Joe (*laughing*) Flattery will get you somewhere. Oblige the lady, Jube. If she bites you, I'll shoot her.
Jubilee (*disgustedly*) Cor ...

Jubilee gets off the stool and stands in front of Mrs Brockett. He holds up his arms—still with the gun in one hand. Mrs Brockett unconcernedly spreads the pullover across him

Mrs Brockett Not far out. (*She prods him with a forefinger*) Breathe in a moment. Mm. Now out again. Thanks. Much obliged. (*She sits down and resumes knitting*)

Jubilee shakes his head, returns to his stool and picks up the magazine

Joe See? Not in the least worried. Or pretends she isn't.
Clem You don't expect them to sit in a row and shiver.
Joe It's the arrogance. They're right. We're wrong. So ignore us.
Clem It doesn't matter, love. In two days we'll be in another place—happier and richer than they'll ever be. (*He kisses her lightly on the cheek*) Forget them.
Joe I'd like to give them something to remember us by. (*Slowly*) Wonder if we could set them against each other? Break up that united front.
Clem It isn't worth it.
Joe Might be interesting to try. We've got a few hours to go yet.
Clem No.
Joe (*not listening*) Now—where's their weakness? Not the girl. The wailer's nothing. The old girl's gutsy, but I think that's more because she's ignorant. Can't see what's under her nose.
Clem She's a countrywoman. Stubborn.

Joe is now more or less talking to herself

Joe The magistrate cow. What's under her nose is the only thing she *can* see—and not even that if she decides not to.
Clem Hester?
Joe Ah, yes. Ma'am. Have you spotted something about ma'am? She doesn't ask questions. But if you don't watch it, you find you're giving her the answers. For free.
Clem That's the trained academic mind.
Joe No. Ma'am's not the weakness. That leaves our Henry. (*Laughing*) Of course. Because he's the one who's really afraid of me ...
Clem Oh, come *on* ...
Joe He thinks he ought to tackle me. Professionally. Show me the error of my ways. But he can't. I'm too strong for him, and he knows it. (*Laughing*) Our Henry. You know, I shouldn't be surprised if—deep down—he fancies me.
Clem Joe ...
Joe Dear Henry. His conscience must be giving him hell. Perhaps we can do something about it ...

Julia stands up. She taps a tuning-fork on the table. The group begin to sing, very quietly and in harmony, the first verse of "Holy Night". Mrs Brockett and Mrs Stevens move from the windowseat to join in. Julia conducts

The Group "Holy night, stilly night . . ."*
Joe Stop it!

Joe starts to move. Clem stops her

Clem No. Let them.

The group end the verse

The Group ". . . sleep in heavenly peace——"
Clem (*clapping*) Bravo!

Julia bows ironically

Mrs Stevens Now you can't say I wasn't good in that.
Julia It wasn't so difficult, was it? Once you were singing the right song . . .
Mrs Stevens It's *not* a song. It's a *carol*—you ought to know that.
Joe All *right*! You've had your fun. Just don't do it again, that's all.

Matty suddenly blazes up

Matty Why should we all sit round waiting for you! We need something to *do*——
Joe Something to do, eh? Very well, sweetie. You *shall* do something. All of you. We'll have a working-squad. (*She gets up and opens the inner door*) You can clear the dishes and wash them up. And while you're about it, you can clean down that kitchen. Thoroughly. Leave it all nice and clean for the owners on Monday. And then you can cut some sandwiches for our journey . . .
Julia I will not . . .
Joe Oh, yes, you will. (*She brings the gun from her pocket*) Besides, it will be a nice Christian act, won't it, Henry? I'm sure you ladies want to please your vicar. All your handmaidens, Henry. Think of that.
Matty (*in a very low voice*) She's *foul* . . .
Joe Come on. One or two of you look as though you don't soil your hands very often. (*Suddenly*) Move!

They start getting up. Mrs Brockett rolls up her knitting

Mrs Brockett I don't mind a bit of a change. From what I saw of that kitchen, it could do with sorting.
Joe You'll sort it all right, grandma. With three guns in the back of you. Out!

Joe motions Mrs Stevens out past her

Mrs Stevens goes through the inner door

Mrs Brockett puts her knitting in her bag

* See Production Note.

Act II

(*To Mrs Brockett*) And if you've any clever ideas about throwing water in someone's face—forget it.
Mrs Brockett I was hoping there might be some flyspray.

Mrs Brockett goes briskly out after Mrs Stevens

Joe gestures to Jubilee

Jubilee follows Mrs Brockett

Joe (*calling through the door*) Someone pass out that big tray.

Mrs Brockett hands Joe a tray through the door

(*To Julia*) Here—you. Mrs Music . . .

Julia takes the tray and returns to the table. She, Henry and Hester clear the dishes, etc., on to it. Matty goes to the counter

Matty Is there a little tray, please?

Clem finds a small tray under the counter and gives it to her. She takes it back to the table

Joe Hurry up, there—don't be all night.

Henry takes the loaded tray out. Julia and Hester follow. Joe goes out after them

Matty puts the last things, cruets, etc., on the tray, puts the tray on a chair and takes off the cloth. Clem moves down to her

I'll give you a hand.

They fold the cloth. Matty takes it to the counter and returns. She and Clem reach for the small tray together. Their hands meet. For a second, they look at each other. Matty straightens up

Matty (*very quietly*) You can't really love her.
Clem (*smiling*) You don't understand, little kitty-cat. Joe's all right.
Matty She'll destroy you.
Clem Don't be dramatic.
Matty She's evil.
Clem She's strong. I need someone strong.
Matty It needn't be her. Please, Clem . . .
Clem I told you. You don't understand.
Matty Explain it to me.

Clem looks at her. Still smiling, he shakes his head

Why not?
Clem You'll get hurt.
Matty I'll risk that . . .
Clem No. You go back to your university and get a good degree. And

marry a nice little bloke with a nice little job who'll give you nice little kids——
Matty Clem . . .
Clem —because you're a nice little kitty-cat—(*he puts a finger under her chin and tilts up her face*)——
Matty (*whispering*) Clem . . .
Clem —who doesn't understand. (*He kisses her very gently full on the lips*)

Joe enters through the inner door. She stands looking at them for a second, then goes out, as—

the CURTAIN *falls*

ACT III

The same. One hour later

When the CURTAIN *rises the room is empty. The curtains are drawn close. Joe enters from the inner door carrying a canvas haversack. She puts it on the stool on the upstage end of the counter, looks at her watch, then goes to the radio and switches it on*

Announcer's Voice ... six o'clock news. (*Pause*) The search continues for John Kevin Jubilee who escaped from Colnbrook prison early this morning. It is thought Jubilee may have been joined by Alan Clement Prior who was associated with him in the Alresford robbery. Prior was released last year after serving two years. Anyone having information as to the whereabouts of either of these men is asked to telephone the Chief Constable ...

Joe switches off. She goes behind the counter, takes the gun from her pocket and lays it ready to hand on top. She takes various packets from the shelves, cigarettes, chocolate, crisps and tins of Coca-Cola, etc., and stacks them on the counter. She goes to the other side of the counter, opens the haversack on the upstage stool and begins to fill it methodically

Mrs Stevens enters from the inner door carrying a large dish of sandwiches and goes behind the counter

Mrs Stevens Is there any mustard there? These sandwiches are ham. (*She goes and looks on the shelves*)
Joe Don't bother.
Mrs Stevens You can't have a ham sandwich without mustard. (*She finds a knife and jar on the shelves*) Do you mind if I do it here?
Joe (*intent on packing*) Suit yourself.

Mrs Stevens opens each sandwich and spreads it carefully, talking in her high-pitched voice

Mrs Stevens It's English mustard—they don't have any French. French is really so much better with a good sugar-cured ham—do you mind it—the English mustard, I mean?
Joe I told you. Suit yourself.
Mrs Stevens But I'm not going to eat them.
Joe Oh, for heaven's sake—I don't *care*.
Mrs Stevens Or would you rather have none at all? I mean—I think ...
Joe Look—just get on with it.
Mrs Stevens Suit yourself.

Joe looks up sharply—then resumes packing. Mrs Stevens goes on with the sandwiches. She begins to sing in a small but quite tuneful voice

"Haste, haste, shepherds and neighbours, shadows are falling, music is calling. Haste, haste, leaving your labours, dance on the gr-reen at the end of the da-a-ay." (*She breaks off*) I *can* sing in tune, you know. *She* keeps saying I can't, but I can.

Joe does not answer

(*Confidentially*) I wasn't going to do these sandwiches. I thought I shouldn't for someone like you. But then *she* said I shouldn't. She said "Phyllis, you are morally obliged *not* to assist these people." (*Simply*) So I did them.

Joe Good.

Mrs Stevens (*complacently*) I did them specially well, too. Buttered right up to the edges. Here—taste.

Joe (*intent on packing*) Not now.

Mrs Stevens Go on. (*She spears a sandwich on the knife and holds it almost under Joe's nose*)

Joe Oh, hell . . . (*She grabs the sandwich and takes a bite, hardly stopping packing. With her mouth full*) Very nice. (*She pauses, swallows and takes another bite*) Mm. They *are* good. Very good indeed.

Mrs Stevens (*nodding*) It's the mustard.

Mrs Stevens finds a sheet of wrapping paper under the counter, spreads it on top and places the sandwiches on it. Joe finishes packing and puts the bag on the floor by the stool. She sits on the stool and takes another sandwich. A calculating expression comes into her face

Joe That woman—Mrs Music. You're afraid of her, aren't you?

Mrs Stevens She upsets me.

Joe But at the moment *I* don't seem to be upsetting you. Why?

Mrs Stevens I was very afraid of you at first. I mean—the guns and everything. But I don't think you'll kill us. And you've done wrong and you'll get caught in the end, so I don't see why I have to be afraid of you in the meantime.

Joe (*laughing*) Well, bully for you. Here—give me one more. (*She takes a sandwich and eats*) You're right. The mustard does make a difference.

Mrs Stevens I read once that a *very* tiny scrap of garlic can be added, but I didn't like it. Even a few grains seems to spoil the ham. (*Earnestly*) I think it stimulates the saliva too much.

Joe Got it all worked out, haven't you?

Mrs Stevens *They* think I'm stupid. But there are some things I know about. And cooking's one of them. I'm a *very* good cook.

Joe (*lazily*) Why do they think you're stupid?

Mrs Stevens Well, I've never been a *pushing* kind of person. My husband did everything. And when he died—not so long ago—I couldn't cope. Not at first. I got more and more worried. And then they said I had a breakdown.

Joe And did you?

Mrs Stevens Not really—I just needed time to adjust. And people *harried me*. They tried to help in the wrong way.

Joe Wrong way?

Act III

Mrs Stevens They said: "Now, Phyllis, don't *brood*. Pull yourself *together*. Be *careful*. You know what you *are*." Well, I know what I am, all right, but their idea seems to be different.
Joe You know what you should have done?
Mrs Stevens No?
Joe You should have looked them straight in the eye, and . . . (*She leans over and whispers*)
Mrs Stevens Oh—I couldn't. They'd be hurt . . .
Joe *They'd* be hurt . . . !
Mrs Stevens Yes. They mean so well. That Mrs King—she really thought it would do me good to join her choir.
Joe Two or three dirty weekends would have been a damn sight better.
Mrs Stevens I do enjoy it when we're all singing together. Then she taps with her little stick for silence and picks on me for being wrong. (*Her voice rises a little*) I do NOT sing out of tune!
Joe (*laughing*) All right, all right. I believe you.

Mrs Stevens finishes wrapping. She puts the dish, mustard and knife tidily under the counter, and pushes the packet towards Joe

Mrs Stevens I think these will keep fresh till you want them.
Joe Ta. Have a fag? (*She offers a packet*)
Mrs Stevens (*taking a cigarette*) Yes, I will. (*Laughing*) That's another thing she'll say I shouldn't do.
Joe Take a cigarette from me?
Mrs Stevens Well—it is *stolen*, isn't it? (*Laughing*) I think I'll enjoy it all the more for that.
Joe You're learning. Here . . . (*She gives her a light*)
Mrs Stevens (*suddenly*) I'll tell you something. Something I've never told anyone—but I'll never see you again, so it doesn't matter.
Joe Well?
Mrs Stevens On the telly. I like the violent bits—where they bring out the guns and talk out of the sides of their mouths. (*Imitating the accent*) "C'mon, men! Let's go . . ." (*She has kept the cigarette in the corner of her mouth. It makes her cough. She drops it on the floor and puts her foot on it*) You don't do that, do you? Talk out of the sides of your . . .

Joe yawns

Joe We're not so bloody silly. (*She bends down to put the sandwiches in the haversack*)
Mrs Stevens And I've always wanted to handle one of these . . .

Joe jerks up—too late. Mrs Stevens has picked up the gun

Joe Put that down!

Joe reaches, but Mrs Stevens backs to the shelves, putting the counter between them

Mrs Stevens It's lighter than I thought. (*Interestedly*) Is that where you put the bullets in?
Joe I'll show you . . .
Mrs Stevens No, I can see. What's this little catch—oh, it pulls up . . .

Joe backs to the top end of the counter

Joe Don't touch that . . . !

There is a click, then Mrs Stevens raises the gun and points it across the room. Joe backs to the windowseat. She raises her voice, but speaks steadily

    Jubilee! (*Pause*) Jubilee . . . !
Jubilee (*off*) Hullo?
Joe In here. Move . . . !

Jubilee enters by the inner door, gun in hand. Henry, Hester, Julia and Matty appear in the doorway, with Clem behind

Jubilee Flaming . . .

He takes a step down. Joe checks him

Joe Hold it. She's got the safety-catch off.

An uncertain pause—then Julia pushes past, strides down, and turns to face Mrs Stevens. Hester and Henry move quietly down beside her

Julia Phyllis—GIVE THAT TO ME AT ONCE!
Joe (*quietly*) She'd better not.
Hester Phyllis, dear—I think you should let Henry have that . . .
Henry I should *rather* like to look at it . . .
Julia (*to Joe, furiously*) What do you mean by giving her that . . .
Mrs Stevens (*placidly*) She didn't give it to me. I took it.
Julia T-took it . . . ?
Mrs Stevens Yes. I just picked it up. That's more than you would have done, isn't it? I heard you telling Henry.
Julia Very brave of you. Now—hand it over.

Mrs Stevens raises the gun in both hands and points it at Julia. She is perfectly relaxed and conversational

Mrs Stevens Stop bullying me. You're always bullying me.
Julia I have *never* . . .
Mrs Stevens Yes, you have. You—you *loom*. You think I can't sing in tune. And you tell people I'm stupid.
Hester (*quietly*) Phyllis . . .
Mrs Stevens (*placidly*) I *liked* being in your old choir until you started picking on me. I liked people until you made them laugh at me. Well, it's got to stop.

Joe begins to laugh silently

    I know you don't mean to be unkind. It's just your way. But it's got to *stop*.
Julia Now, Phyllis . . .
Mrs Stevens I shall stay in your choir and I shall sing how I like. And if I stand up a bit later than the others I shall do that, too. And you'll stop telling people I'm stupid. Because I *may* be stupid. And I *may* sing out of tune. (*Pausing*) But it was *me* and not *you* who picked up the gun. (*She raises the gun a little higher*) And if you ever make a fool of

Act III

me again, in any way whatsoever—I shall look you straight in the eye and tell you to get stuffed.

Joe doubles up over the counter

Hester Phyllis . . .
Julia Wait. (*To Mrs Stevens*) You are perfectly right. I had no idea I was upsetting you. As you say, it is my way and it appears it was the wrong way. In future, I promise to treat you with respect and—if you will accept it—friendship.
Mrs Stevens Is that an apology?
Julia It is.
Mrs Stevens And it won't make any difference when I haven't got this?
Julia No.
Mrs Stevens That's all right, then.

Julia's hand goes out

(*To Joe*) Thank you. I don't need that any more. (*She gives the gun to Joe*)
Julia Phyllis . . . !
Mrs Stevens (*suddenly*) I think—I think I'm going to be sick . . .

Hand to mouth, Mrs Stevens runs out through the inner door. Matty, Mrs Brockett and Clem follow

Julia (*furiously*) Did you see that! She had the gun in her hand—and she gave it back—she actually had it in her hand and . . .
Joe Shut up!
Julia You wicked creature! You gave her the gun—you put her up to this —you know she's unbalanced.
Joe She's no more unbalanced than you are. So keep quiet.
Julia I will NOT . . . !
Joe Oh yes, you will.

Joe clicks her safety-catch. Jubilee does the same

You think we won't use these. Well, just don't push your luck. Sit down.

Hester and Henry move to the table. Julia still faces Joe

(*Laughing*) Made you eat dirt, didn't she? And let you off lightly. Me— I'd have had you crawling. On your knees.

Julia stalks away and sits at the downstage end of the table. Joe goes behind the counter and beckons Jubilee over

Joe (*suddenly overcome*) She—she asked me—where the bullets went in . . .
Jubilee Crissake——
Joe That Julia's face! (*Sobering*) She talks about being cruel. I reckon if she'd been on our side she'd have shown us a thing or two.

Mrs Stevens returns from the inner door, followed by Matty, Mrs Brockett and Clem

Mrs Stevens I wasn't sick. I thought I would be, but I wasn't.

Mrs Stevens sits at the top end of the table. Matty sits on the windowseat, takes papers and books from her bag and puts on her spectacles. Mrs Brockett collects her knitting and sits below the table

I should like a cup of coffee.

Joe Well—Mrs Music. You heard what the lady said.

Julia pauses. Then she goes to the counter and pours coffee, which she takes to Mrs Stevens

Mrs Stevens Oh, thank you. (*She sips*) You forgot the sugar. (*She holds out the cup*) Two spoons, please.

Julia tightens her lips, but takes the coffee back for sugar and returns it to Mrs Stevens

Thank you. I hope you didn't mind. Sugar gives you energy, you know.

Julia returns to her seat at the table. Clem joins Joe and Jubilee at the counter

Joe (*quietly*) I just heard the radio. They're on to Clem. And I've had this lot. It should be dark enough by ten. Shall we take a chance?
Jubilee Suits me.
Joe Then how about this. We . . .

They talk with their heads together

Mrs Brockett (*to Mrs Stevens*) Here—come over here and let's get this wool wound. It's not often I have a chance to sit about so long.

Mrs Brockett picks up a hank of wool, urges Mrs Stevens up to the stool by the wall, sits her on it with the wool over her hands and starts winding. Julia angrily lights a cigarette—but the match goes out

Julia Damn . . . !
Hester Calm down, Julia.
Julia That girl was positively gloating—what a situation . . .
Hester I thought you got out of it very well, and with dignity.
Julia Dignity? I have never been so humiliated in my life.
Henry (*quietly*) Mrs Stevens has been humiliated quite a few times.
Julia What do you mean? Oh. Now don't tell me you're on her side . . .
Hester It's not a question of sides. She *has* been through rather a bad time . . .
Julia Everyone goes through bad times. We have to be *firm*—stand up to them . . .
Hester We're not all such strong characters as you. Phyllis can't . . .
Julia Phyllis can't be allowed to sit about wailing. She needs an objective. Something definite. Heaven knows I've done my best.
Henry By making her afraid of you?
Julia (*drily*) She certainly wasn't afraid of me just now.

Hester suddenly begins to laugh quietly. Henry joins in

Act III

Julia Really—it is not funny.
Hester I'm sorry, Julia. My turn to apologize.
Julia (*suddenly*) Perhaps it is. (*Slowly*) When you come to think of it—that little rabbit—standing there with the gun—and telling me—telling me . . .

They all three laugh

(*Sobering*) Tell me—honestly. *Do* I terrify people?
Henry You don't mean to.
Julia But *do* I?
Hester You are inclined to be a bit of a steamroller.
Julia I get *interested*. People are so slow to understand. I have to *push* them—(*slowly*)—is that it?
Henry That's it, Julia.
Julia But it's for their own good. Their own achievement.
Hester Sometimes you forget they have feelings.
Julia I—see. Well, well, I shall have to try and walk more delicately. Otherwise, Phyllis might carry out her threat. (*Laughing*) Just think if she did. The Committee would probably ask me to resign. (*She lights another cigarette from the end of the first*)
Henry (*suddenly*) As a matter of fact, Julia, there *has* been a . . .
Hester (*quietly, but with authority*) Henry . . .

Henry looks at her. She shakes her head

It won't be necessary. Not now.
Julia I wonder how they've got on. Mary is very good of course, but she hasn't quite got the initial *attack*. I have told her over and over again . . . (*She breaks off, looking at them*) You know, this is going to be a bit of a challenge.
Hester I'm sure you'll accept it.
Julia You'll have to keep reminding me, that's all. (*Picking up the score*) Do you think we could possibly find someone somewhere who could do . . .

Julia stops. Everyone looks up, tensing. Jubilee, listening to Joe, has brought out a flick-knife and clicked it open. He sits cleaning his nails

Joe . . . take it across country for the first twelve miles, then we avoid the main roads . . .

The talk becomes inaudible. The others relax

Julia (*steadily*) If we made enquiries we might get someone who could do the double *ostinati* in the "Jubilate" . . .
Hester Now, I wonder if we could coax Tom Brockett—let's have another look . . .

They study the score again

Joe Then we're all agreed?
Jubilee O.K.
Joe Then we'd better organize breaks for rest. You go back there, Jube,

and get a good kip. Clem and I'll hold on here. Call you in about an hour.
Jubilee (*putting away his knife*) Sure. (*He gets up*) But that's it. Ten we go.
Joe Ten we go . . . (*She stops*)

Steps and voices are heard outside the main door. Jubilee takes out his gun and pads to the main door. Clem goes to the inner door. Joe picks up her gun and goes to the window, peering through the extreme edge of the curtain. Laughter is heard, then a hammering on the main door

Man (*off*) Anyone home? Hullo? Anyone there?
Woman (*off*) Oh, come *on*, Ron. It's closed.
Man (*off*) Don't see why. (*Hammering*) Hullo, there!
Woman (*off*) It's late. And it's Saturday. They're closed for the weekend.
Man (*off*) Not that late. And I'm thirsty, I could do with a pot of tea.
Woman (*off*) Well, you're not going to get it. There's no-one there.
Man (*off*) I'm going round the back. Let's see if we can get in. Might be a window open——

Footsteps cross the window to the other side. Clem raises his gun and clicks the catch

Woman (*off, still outside the main door*) No. I'm not traipsing about any more. It's CLOSED! Can't you see the sign. Come on—let's go up to Carlo's . . .
Man (*off*) Oh, all right.

The footsteps move back. There is a final hammering on the main door

Lazy so-and-so's. Saturday an' all . . .

The footsteps move away. There is an outburst of giggling

Woman (*off*) Stop it—can't you! *Ron!* Don't *do* that!

The laughter and steps die away

Matty (*under her breath*) Damn!
Joe Hard luck.

Joe goes behind the counter

Jubilee goes past Clem and out through the inner door

Clem moves across towards the main door. As he passes Matty he pauses and turns back. He picks up a book from the windowseat

Clem Well, look at that. Spivak.
Matty Did you use him?
Clem Use him? Spent my last term keeping him together with Sellotape. Where there's calculus, there's Spivak. (*He picks up a paper*) What's this?
Matty (*quietly*) Just a problem.

Act III

Clem I can see that. What are you trying to do?
Matty Integration by parts. (*Sighing*) I shall never be able to integrate by parts.
Clem Hang about. Let's see. (*He studies the paper*) Oh, I get it. You've got a product of three functions, all of the same variable, and you're asked to perform the integration by parts . . .
Matty That's it.
Clem Well, you're not going to do it that way, love. Here—give us a pencil . . . (*He transfers the gun to his left hand and sits down beside her, making notes and talking inaudibly*)

Joe looks over. She puts down her coffee cup. Hester gets up and crosses to the counter. Julia and Henry are absorbed in the score

Hester (*quietly*) May I drink a cup of coffee with you? (*She helps herself*)

Joe looks at Matty and Clem and back at Hester

Joe I can break it up whenever I like.
Hester So can I. (*She sits on the upstage stool*)
Joe Then why don't you?
Hester Just for the moment they're speaking their own language.
Joe Much good it's done him. (*Abruptly*) You'd like to ask me how it happened, wouldn't you—ma'am?
Hester Only if you would like to tell me.
Joe You don't believe in asking questions.
Hester I don't believe in forcing confidences.
Joe Just as well then, isn't it?
Hester If you think so.
Joe What I think—what I do—isn't your concern. There's a line drawn down the road, ma'am. You're one side and I'm the other. And that's how I like it.
Hester All your life—looking over your shoulder.
Joe (*laughing*) Keeps you on the alert.
Hester You are perhaps—twenty-four?
Joe Twenty-five. What age did they put you out to grass?
Hester At sixty.
Joe And you started—what? Twenty . . . ?
Hester Twenty-two.
Joe Forty-eight years' graft. I'll tell you something, ma'am. I'll be retired next week. At twenty-five.
Hester Indeed?
Joe So long before sixty, I'll be sitting pretty. Very pretty indeed.
Hester And what will you do?
Joe Do?
Hester You will have the most precious thing in the world. Complete control of your own time. What will you do with all those years?
Joe (*laughing*) Nothing.
Hester Nothing.
Joe What you'd call nothing. Look at the world. Lie in the sun. Drink wine. Make love. I bet you haven't done all that.

Hester Most of it.
Joe (*laughing*) Even the love bit?
Hester You will remember we are not exchanging confidences.
Joe I don't believe it. Not your generation.
Hester Yours doesn't have the monopoly of physical experience.
Joe (*scornfully*) You were all afraid. You always played it safe.
Hester There is something to be said for security.
Joe Not me. Too dull. No, ma'am, I'm going to live.
Hester Doing nothing. No. I don't think so.
Joe Why not?
Hester You have too good and too active a brain. I should have liked to have the training of it.
Joe Training for what? To write about bloody clocks?
Hester I can't know, of course. But I can see you as a teacher, an organizer —certainly a leader . . .
Clem (*at the window*) . . . so you simply treat the product of these two as a separate function, and apply the formula in two stages. And we're left with this function—(*scribbling on paper*)—*plus* the constant of integration . . .
Matty Yes—yes, I do see. Thank you——

Hester puts her cup on the counter

Hester (*quietly*) Thank you for talking to me. I hope that getting the things you want will make you happy. (*She goes back to her seat at the table*)
Matty —and that way makes it so much easier . . .
Joe (*harshly*) Clem.

Clem looks up

Over here.

Clem puts the papers down and goes to the counter

It might be as well if the bikes were checked over. Don't want any hold up . . .
Clem I'll do it now.
Joe Go that way. Don't disturb Jube. Oh—and take this out ready. (*She gives Clem the haversack*)

Clem goes to the main door, unbolts it, and exits

Mrs Brockett and Mrs Stevens go to the windowseat. Joe goes to bolt the door behind Clem. Matty gets up and moves to the middle of the room. As Joe turns and moves back, they come face to face

(*Smiling*) Did your sums for you, did he?
Matty He solved a problem—yes.
Joe (*deliberately*) For the little kitty-cat—who doesn't understand?

Matty flinches

Matty He didn't . . .
Joe What do you think?

Act III

Joe goes behind the counter. Matty looks at her, then goes to the chair above the table. Mrs Brockett goes to the counter with her bag

Mrs Brockett This excitement is stepping up my smoking. Are you prepared to sell me ten tipped Woods, Miss?

Joe takes a packet from the shelves

Joe There you are, grandma. (*Laughing*) Have it on me.
Mrs Brockett That I will not. You can't give what isn't yours. Nineteen p. There's twenty. Put it in the till and give me the change.

Mrs Brockett slaps some coins on the counter. Joe puts them in the till and puts a penny on the counter top

Joe Better count it, gran.
Mrs Brockett Certainly. And don't call me gran. If your own grandmother's alive, I reckon you'll have broken her heart.
Joe (*laughing*) Never had a gran, gran. Like Topsy. Just growed.
Julia I'm surprised you should be acquainted with Harriet Beecher Stowe.

Mrs Brockett goes back to the windowseat

Joe Did it for my O-levels.
Julia And no doubt conceived a violent admiration for Simon Legree.

Joe leans her arms along the counter

Joe Shall I tell you what I remember about that book?
Hester Please do.
Joe All the goodies died.
Julia Well?
Joe Henry here would say death is the wages of sin. But the *goodies* died.
Henry They died secure in their faith. History is filled with such people.
Joe While the wicked flourish like the green bay tree. Oh, yes, Henry. I know the odd bit of Holy Writ.
Henry So does the devil.
Joe Is that how you see me, Henry? Horns and a tail? How unkind. Please let me be a nice, very flourishing green bay tree.
Henry You will be what you make yourself. What you are.
Joe (*mocking*) Now's your chance to try and change it. Well?
Henry You are not answerable to me.
Joe Oh, Henry. No sermon? No fire and brimstone?
Henry You're a little out of date.
Joe Really? No more hell? No fiery furnace? What do you preach, then?

Henry does not answer

Come on, Henry. What do you talk about to your tame tabbies on Sunday? Or don't they come? Ah, is that it? No-one comes?

Henry still does not answer

Oh, *poor* Henry. Give up all your poor little life to preach the Gospel. And no-one comes to hear it . . .
Hester (*suddenly*) That is enough. (*Her voice is quiet, but the authority is there. She goes to Joe*)
Joe (*dangerously*) Ma'am . . . ?
Hester I said that is enough. For the rest of the time we are here, you will not speak like that again. To any of us.
Joe Why not?
Hester Because it will not help your own wounds to inflict pain on others.

There is a pause. Joe's face hardens

Henry cannot turn and answer you as you deserve. I can. And if you don't stop this abominable behaviour, I shall . . .
Joe (*softly*) You'll what—ma'am . . . ?
Hester I shall slap you across your face so hard that you will remember it all those fifty years you boast of.

Joe clicks off the safety-catch

Oh, yes. You can use that. I don't doubt it. And then—in prison or out of it—you'll look back over your shoulder for the rest of your life.

They look at each other

Joe (*in a very low voice*) Just don't provoke me, that's all. Just don't . . .

The telephone rings. They all react. Joe backs through the lower end of the counter and pulls the lead viciously from its socket. Hester goes back to the table. No-one moves or speaks as Joe takes a pack of cigarettes from the shelves and lights one

Julia (*suddenly*) Does anyone feel like more coffee?
Matty I don't think I shall ever want to *look* at a cup of coffee as long as I live.
Hester Hold on, darling. It won't be long now.
Julia And I wonder where they're going, and why.
Matty I'd rather not know. I just want—never to see them again.

Joe stretches and yawns

(*Bitterly*) Don't you ever sleep?
Joe Not on the job. (*She strolls down smoking, and stands by the table*) You don't all realize how lucky you are.
Julia Lucky . . . !
Joe We could have shut you all up back there, taken out the light bulb and let you sweat it out in the dark. Easier for us, too—no need for guns.
Matty Why didn't you?
Joe Because we're not the desperate thugs you make out. We're human.
Matty Human . . .
Joe Human enough to let you stay loose, drink your coffee and smoke your fags. And abuse us just because we're outside the Establishment. (*She pulls out a chair, turns it and sits with her arms across the back*)

Act III

Actually, I believe you hate us more than we hate you. Only you won't admit it.

Hester Hating us at all is your mistake.

Joe Is it? D'you know what you godbodies do to people? Have you ever thought about it?

Hester Tell us.

Julia I don't want to hear.

Matty I do.

Joe All you want to hear, little kitty-cat, is about Clem. Yes?

Matty I don't . . .

Joe Be honest. You're dying to know.

Matty Not from you.

Joe You'll hear it from me and like it. You'll hear exactly what you've done to Clem.

Matty Please . . .

Joe (*not listening*) He's done the lot, hasn't he? University. Degree. Brilliant mathematician. Full of promise. So the damn fool gets a job as an accountant. In a big company.

Julia What's wrong with that?

Joe He sits every day of his life in a long room. With twenty desks, twenty reading-lamps, and nineteen other poor little sods who're going to be accountants, too. The only difference between that and prison is that they let them out for an hour to eat and allow them home to sleep.

Julia There are other forms of employment.

Joe That's what Clem thought. So he went for a store manager. Trainee. Longer hours but not so cramped. Plenty of people around. It was quite good. For a year.

Julia He had obviously no staying power.

Joe He was transferred to another store. Promotion. On the first morning, his manager greeted him. He said: "So you're one of those bloody graduates? Well, watch out. I don't like them in my store."

Julia He could still have made a change.

Joe He had decided he liked the work. He wasn't going to be beaten. That was his mistake.

Hester Or his determination.

Joe His mistake. That manager was out to break him. One day it went just too far. Clem hit him.

Julia Unfortunate, but not necessarily a disaster.

Joe He broke his jaw.

Matty Oh, no!

Joe Oh, yes. And the Company prosecuted.

Julia He could hardly get more than probation.

Joe Yes—you'd know that bit, wouldn't you? Young man, university, good record. Such a pity. Now just don't do anything wrong for eighteen months, lick the boots of your probation officer and everything will be all right. (*Slowly*) That's how we met. In Court.

Julia (*politely*) Were you also in the dock?

Joe Sorry to disappoint you. I was swearing to an alibi.

Julia I hope it stood up.

Joe Oh, yes. It had been worked out very carefully. (*Slowly*) I saw Clem. He looked—pretty awful. I spoke to him, and then I took him out for a drink. (*She looks full at Matty*) We ended up in bed. We've been together ever since.

Julia He seems to have gone downhill very quickly. Probation is hardly a life sentence.

Joe Think not? Well, tell me—Mrs Music—have you ever tried getting a job with that against you?

Julia With the help of a good officer it is perfectly possible . . .

Joe Don't make me laugh. Why did you leave your last job? I was sacked. Why? I broke my boss's jaw. I'm on probation. Oh, yes, I do have a first-class degree in mathematics—thank you, good morning. That's the Establishment. That's what it does to people.

Hester What has it done to you?

Joe I thought you never asked questions.

Hester I am asking this one.

Joe laughs, gets up and pushes the chair back against the table

Joe No, ma'am. I think I'll just remain a mystery . . .

Police sirens are heard in the distance. Joe jumps up. Clem hammers on the main door

Clem (*off, outside the main door*) Joe! Joe! Open up . . .!

Joe opens the main door

   Clem falls in

I think something's up. Police cars—a whole lot of them . . .

Joe Easy! Listen . . .

The sirens sound nearer, but still some distance away

It's all right. Probably been an accident somewhere.

Clem I don't like it. Let's get going.

Joe Look—don't panic. How could they know we're here?

Julia (*triumphantly*) Because I told them.

Joe comes slowly to the middle of the room

Joe (*quietly*) What the hell are you talking about?

Julia The message I gave to my colleagues on the telephone.

Joe slowly raises the gun, and clicks the safety-catch

Joe Start talking. Fast.

Julia With the greatest pleasure. I told my colleague to consult Lord Hamlyn about a score. He has the finest collection of church scores in the country. That is why he is so interested in choirs . . .

Joe Get on with it!

Julia I mentioned a score of Judas Maccabaeus. Incidentally, that is an oratorio by Handel—about which you will not understand . . .

Act III

Joe I'll give you two minutes to get to the point.
Julia The point is extremely simple. Our choir has never used that score. That would be the first indication of something unusual. There is an aria in it. You may remember—I mentioned aria forty-five. I told them particularly to note the first line. And do you know what that first line is? (*She holds the pause*) It is "Sound an alarm".
Joe Sound——
Julia (*singing*)* "Sound an alarm, sound an alarm, Your silver trumpets sound——" The inference is obvious provided they had the intelligence to check the score——

The sirens sound a little nearer

—which apparently they had.
Matty Oh—Julia . . .
Henry Well done! Well done!
Joe You're bluffing. You've just made it all up.
Julia You heard me on the telephone. You didn't call me Mrs Music for nothing!
Matty And you can't risk it. Either you go while you can. Or you wait and take a chance.
Joe We'll take the chance . . .
Clem No, Joe. Remember what's at stake . . .

Joe pauses. Then she nods

Joe All right. Get Jubilee. (*Calling*) Jube . . . !

Clem runs out through the inner door

Along that wall, all of you. Move. (*To Mrs Brockett and Mrs Stevens*) And you two. I said move!

They all line up behind the table

What the hell . . . (*Calling*) JUBE . . . !

Clem enters from the inner door, carrying a gun

Clem Joe . . .
Joe What is it? Where's Jubilee?

Jubilee enters from the inner door, carrying a whisky bottle, his hat on the back of his head. He is not too unsteady, his speech is not too slurred, but he is coldly, dangerously drunk

Jubilee Hullo, Joe. How are you?
Joe Oh, my God . . .
Jubilee C-cheers! (*He takes a drink, wipes his mouth on the back of his hand, and sits on the windowseat*)
Joe Jube, what have you . . .

* See Production Note.

Jubilee (*grinning*) Been having myself a ball. A b-beautiful, beautiful ball. Haven't felt so good for f-four b-bloody years. (*He drinks again*)
Joe Get them locked up, Clem. (*Pausing*) Where are the keys?
Clem In the cupboard door.
Joe How much has he had?
Clem That's the second bottle.
Joe All right. I'll deal with it. Get them out. You—all of you—move!

All but Joe and Jubilee file out through the inner door past Clem

Clem puts the gun on the end of the counter

Clem He left it on the floor.

Clem goes out through the inner door

Joe Jubilee...
Jubilee (*happily*) Have a drink.
Joe How the hell did you get that?
Jubilee In cupboard. Where you locked it away from me. Locked it away from me, didn't you. Bossy bitch. Why?
Joe I...
Jubilee Don't say you didn't. I know you did. (*Taking another drink*) The wog told me.
Joe The wog!
Jubilee Yes. Nice little wog. Asked me to let her out. Toilet. Said I would. Locked her in again. Then she said—now I'll do you a good turn. You got keys. Whisky in cupboard. She doesn't want you to have it. (*Suddenly angry*) Flaming hell you didn't. Why not?
Joe Now, Jube...
Jubilee Doing everything, aren't you? Think you're Mister Big. Well, you're flaming not.
Joe Jube, don't waste time. The police are on their way. They know we're here.

Jubilee gets up

Jubilee They can't know.
Joe Listen.

The sirens come nearer, then stop

Jubilee They've gone. Flaming fuzz.
Joe When they close in, they switch off. Jube, don't be a fool. We've got to get going.
Jubilee Then we'll take the car.

Clem comes in from the inner door. He drops the bunch of keys on the end of the counter

Joe You know we can't take that car.
Clem We'll have to. He can never stay on a bike.

Act III

Joe (*savage for the first time*) The fool! The crazy blasted fool!
Jubilee You shut up. We'll take the car. I got the keys. (*He brings the keys from his pocket*)
Joe All right. We'll take the car. Give Clem the keys.
Jubilee I'm driving.
Joe You can't.
Jubilee Why not?
Joe You're drunk.
Jubilee (*dangerously*) Who says I'm drunk?
Joe No time to argue. Give Clem the keys.
Jubilee If you want to know where the money is, you got to come with me.
Joe We know that. But Clem's driving. (*She raises her gun*)
Clem (*warningly*) Joe ...
Joe Cool it, Jube. You'll do as I say.
Jubilee (*grinning*) I will? Why?
Joe You haven't got your gun.

Jubilee pauses. He throws the bottle on the windowseat. He puts his hand in his pocket

So be sensible. Let's go ...

Jubilee's hand comes out of his pocket—with the flick-knife ready

Clem (*whispering*) I warned you.
Jubilee (*quietly*) You want to play it rough?
Clem Careful. He's an expert.
Joe All right, Jube. Put that away.
Jubilee Eh?
Joe Put it away. It's a kid's toy. Here ...

Joe picks up the gun and throws it at Jubilee. Instinctively his left hand goes up to catch it. Joe moves in, grabbing at his arm. Clem runs forward

Clem Joe!

Jubilee's right arm comes down. Clem staggers against the counter. Jubilee runs out through the main door

Joe Jubilee!

Joe runs out after Jubilee

(*Off*) Jubilee ...!

Clem slides slowly along the counter to the middle of it. He stands braced on his hands and rigid arms. Slowly he pulls a handkerchief from his pocket, wads it on the counter with one hand and slides it under his coat. He braces himself again with both hands on the counter. A car is heard revving up violently. It roars away

Joe runs in through the main door and straight across to the inner door, putting the gun in her pocket

He's gone. The bastard wouldn't wait. We'll take the bikes—hurry . . .

Joe exits through the inner door

Clem is still. Then he slides slowly away from the counter until only his hands grasp the top. They gradually loosen. He slides to the floor, resting against the counter, his head lolling on his chest

Joe runs back and across to the main door. She has put on her overalls and is zipping them up, her helmet slung on her arm

Hurry—for God's sake . . . (*She turns at the main door*) Clem—come ON—(*pausing*)—Clem . . . ? (*She stops. She drops her helmet on the windowseat and kneels beside Clem*) Clem . . . ?

Joe lifts Clem's head. It falls back. She gets up, goes to the main door and bolts it. She finds his gun and Jubilee's on the floor, and pockets one, then takes the keys from the counter

Joe runs out through the inner door

Pause. Clem moves slightly once

Joe returns and stands back, motioning the others past her at gun point. Julia, Matty and Henry enter and kneel by Clem. Julia supports him against her. Henry kneels downstage, masking Clem. Lina runs in, looks at Clem, and runs out. Mrs Brockett enters with Mrs Stevens

Mrs Brockett (*quietly, to Mrs Stevens*) You come here with me, dear. They'll tell us if there's anything we can do.

Mrs Brockett and Mrs Stevens sit on the windowseat

Lina runs in with a big towel

They start to remove Clem's jacket and wrap the towel tightly round his chest

Hester enters from the inner door

Joe takes Hester down below the table

Hester It was Jubilee?

Joe nods. Henry crosses to them

Henry I'm sorry . . .
Joe What do you mean?
Henry There's nothing anyone can do.

Act III

Joe (*blankly*) Nothing . . .? You don't know what you're talking about. Phone for an ambulance . . . (*She stops, realizing*)
Henry It wouldn't be any use. The knife went through . . .
Matty Henry—he's trying to say something . . .

Henry goes and kneels by Clem. They spread his jacket over him. Joe runs to the main door and reaches for the bolt

Hester (*quietly*) Joe.

Joe turns

It's too late.
Joe They've got nothing on me. No record. If Jubilee doesn't talk, I could get clear . . .
Hester No.
Joe I know all the roads. I'll make it . . . (*She reaches for the bolt again*)
Hester Go and look out of the window.

Joe swings round. She goes to the window and lifts the curtain. The glare of headlights is seen outside. Joe drops the curtain

Joe runs out through the inner door

Henry (*moving to Hester*) Where's she gone?
Hester To try the back way. It isn't any use . . .

A man's voice is heard off, speaking through a loud hailer

Policeman's Voice (*off*) John Jubilee. Clement Prior. We know you are in there. Come out slowly with your hands above your heads. Repeat— come out slowly with your hands above your heads . . .
Henry I'll let them in. (*He turns to go to the main door*)
Hester No, Henry.
Henry But Hester—it's *over* . . .
Hester (*quietly*) She has to do it herself.

Henry looks at her blankly. Suddenly he reacts violently

Henry No! No—she's evil—the sword of the Lord and of Gideon—let them take her . . .
Hester Henry!

Henry stops. He is shaking. He pulls out his handkerchief and wipes his forehead

Henry (*quietly*) I'm sorry—forgive me——

Joe runs in through the inner door, slams it, and stands with her back against it

Would you come here a moment, please?

Joe comes into the room

He's asking for you.
Joe (*abruptly*) No.
Henry There isn't very much time . . .
Joe No.
Henry How *can* you . . . ?
Matty Henry . . .

Henry crosses and kneels by Clem's feet

Joe (*quietly*) Poor little basket. He wouldn't have made it, anyway. He's too . . .

Matty rises and comes to Joe

Matty He wants you.

Joe shakes her head

For pity's sake—don't you feel *anything*?
Joe (*suddenly*) Feel? What do *you* know about it? What could you ever have done for him?
Matty I . . .
Joe You stupid little nothing! Could you ever hold a man in your arms and make him strong? No. Never. That's what I did. I made him strong.
Matty Then help him now. *Please* . . .
Joe He told you himself. You don't understand.

Matty goes and stands looking down at Clem

Hester Why does it have to be this way?
Joe Because I don't want to remember.
Policeman's Voice (*off*) Attention please—attention please! John Jubilee has been apprehended. Repeat—John Jubilee has been apprehended. Alan Prior and the girl called Joe—come out with your hands above your heads . . .
Hester (*gently*) Stop running, Joe.
Joe I . . .
Hester Stop running.

Hester holds out her hand. Joe pauses. Then she laughs shortly. She raises the gun in a mocking salute

Joe Ma'am. (*She puts the gun in Hester's hand, goes to the main door, and reaches for the bolt*)
Clem (*faintly*) Joe . . .

Joe goes rigid, her back to the room. Matty looks over at her. Then she kneels down and eases Clem from Julia into her own arms

Matty (*quietly*) Yes, Clem . . .

Joe opens the door. She stands in the light of the headlamps

Policeman's Voice (*off*) Come out with your hands above your heads. Repeat—come out with your hands above your heads.

Act III

Joe raises her hands and goes out through the main door

Clem tries feebly to touch Matty's face. She holds his hand against her cheek

Clem (*very faintly*) Joe ...
Matty (*steadily*) Yes, Clem. I'm here. (*She cradles him in her arms*)

Henry stands up

Henry Almighty God, Father of our Lord Jesus Christ, who desireth not the death of a sinner, but rather that he may turn from his wickedness—and live ...

CURTAIN

FURNITURE AND PROPERTY LIST

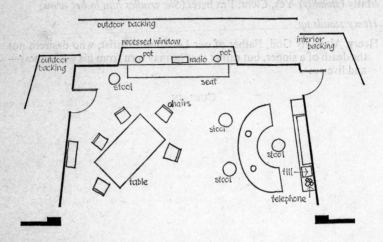

ACT I

SCENE 1

On stage: Large table. *On it:* ashtray
          Counter. *On top:* two-jug Cona apparatus, 2 ashtrays, matches. *Underneath, on shelves:* 12 cups, 12 saucers, 6 mugs; 6 teaspoons, sugar-bowl and spoon; 1 large tray set ready with 6 knives, 6 forks, 6 dessert spoons, 6 side-plates, cruet; small tray set ready with 6 wine-glasses, 6 red paper napkins; 6 extra glasses on shelves, red-and-white-check tablecloth, small bill pad with carbon and pencil attached; jar of mustard and spreading-knife; sheets of greaseproof wrapping-paper; milk and coffee in jugs to replenish Cona when necessary. *On shelves behind, from floor to ceiling:* cigarettes; matches, packets of crisps, jars of coffee and sweets, boxes of chocolates, minerals, Coca-cola cans—sufficient to make a proper trade display. *On shelf level with counter top:* small drawer-till with notes and change, telephone with lead loosely connected to floor downstage

5 stacking-chairs
4 stools
On window: Open Shut sign, reading OPEN
On windowsill: 2 pots of red geraniums, small radio
Below window: upholstered seat
On walls: handwritten menus in slot-frame, a few coloured advertisements as dressing
Window curtains (practical)

The Restless Evil 61

Off stage: Hand-gun, cigarettes, lighter, bunch of keys **(Joe)**
Hand-gun **(Jubilee)**
Hand-gun, cigarettes, lighter **(Clem)**
Waiter's striped jacket **(Clem)**

Personal: **Hester:** handbag, scarf, bunch of car keys, wrist-watch
Henry: wallet with notes and change, wrist-watch
Julia: light briefcase with music score, tuning-fork, matches, cigarettes
Mrs Brockett: handbag with cigarettes, matches, small change
Mrs Stevens: handbag, handkerchief
Matty: shoulder-bag with cigarettes, lighter, notebook, scribbling-pad, pencils, large hard-backed text-book, spectacles
Joe: wrist-watch

Scene 2

Strike: Plates and cutlery on to large tray for **Lina**

Set: *On table:* 3 coffee cups and saucers, 3 wine-glasses, wine bottle—half full and uncorked, music score from **Julia**'s bag
On counter: 2 glasses half full, for **Joe** and **Jubilee**, opened can of Coca-cola, 3 clean glasses by Cona apparatus
On windowseat: **Matty**'s shoulder-bag, books, papers, etc.

Off stage: Large tray **(Clem)**

ACT II

Strike: *From table:* everything except music score and ashtray
From counter: everything except ashtray and matches

Set: Sign to read OPEN
Check sufficient cups and saucers under counter
Check small tray ready under counter
Refill Cona with coffee and milk if necessary

Off stage: Large tray with 3 plates of food, 3 knives, 3 forks, cruet **(Lina)**
Dish of potatoes **(Joe)**
Large tray (for **Mrs Brockett** to hand to **Joe**)
Large brown carrier-bag, lettered in black BIGGS' BACON, containing front half of man's sweater on needles, hanks of wool, tape-measure, knitting-pattern, rolled magazine sticking out **(Jubilee)**

Personal: **Jubilee:** handkerchief or rag for cleaning gun, flick-knife

ACT III

Strike: *From table:* everything except ashtray and score
From counter: everything except ashtrays
From chair: small tray

Set: Curtains drawn closely across windows
Check sufficient cups under counter
Refill Cona apparatus if necessary

Off stage: Large haversack **(Joe)**
Large plate of sandwiches **(Mrs Stevens)**
Empty whisky bottle **(Jubilee)**
Bunch of keys **(Clem)**
Large towel **(Lina)**
Jubilee's gun **(Clem)** * An extra gun should be used

Personal: **Jubilee:** flick-knife

*See Production Note.

LIGHTING PLOT

Property fittings required: nil
Interior. A café. The same scene throughout

ACT I. Day

To open: General effect of summer sunshine
No cues

ACT II. Day

To open: As Act I
No cues

ACT III. Evening

To open: Curtains closed, lighting slightly subdued

Cue 1	**Hester:** ". . . look out of the window." *Full spotlight on window as* **Joe** *pulls curtains aside*	(Page 57)
Cue 2	**Joe** closes curtains over window *Snap off spotlight*	(Page 57)
Cue 3	**Joe** opens main door and looks out *Spotlight immediately full on* **Joe**	(Page 58)
Cue 4	**Joe** exits *Fade spotlight to background lighting*	(Page 59)

EFFECTS PLOT

ACT I

Cue 1	As CURTAIN rises *Music from radio*	(Page 1)
Cue 2	When CURTAIN up *Two motor-cycles arriving and stopping*	(Page 1)
Cue 3	Lina turns off radio *Music off*	(Page 1)
Cue 4	As JUBILEE enters *Police siren in distance—approaches then fades*	(Page 1)
Cue 5	Joe turns on radio *Announcer's voice on radio*	(Page 5)
Cue 6	Jubilee turns on radio *Announcer's voice, then music*	(Page 8)
Cue 7	Lina: "Outside. On left." *Car in distance, approaches, fades*	(Page 9)
Cue 8	Jubilee: "... doing something to that table." *Car in distance, arriving*	(Page 10)
Cue 9	Joe: "Yes, Jube, that's how it is." *Car draws up and stops*	(Page 10)
Cue 10	Joe: "Watch it, lover boy..." *Car door slams*	(Page 10)

ACT II

Cue 11	Joe: "Let them sweat it out..." *Car engine starts and revs*	(Page 23)
Cue 12	Joe: "... stay where you are." *Car drives away*	(Page 23)
Cue 13	Clem: "... cold hard world waiting outside." *Telephone bell rings*	(Page 27)

ACT III

Cue 14	Joe turns on radio *Announcer's voice on radio*	(Page 39)
Cue 15	Joe: "... don't provoke me, that's all." *Telephone bell rings, continue until* Joe *pulls out lead*	(Page 50)
Cue 16	Joe: "... just remain a mystery." *Sirens faintly in distance*	(Page 52)
Cue 17	Joe: "Easy. Listen." *Sirens slightly louder, then fade*	(Page 52)

Cue 18	**Julia:** "... intelligence to check the score——" *Sirens a little louder, then fading*	(Page 53)
Cue 19	**Jubilee:** "They can't know." *Sirens start up, nearer, rising slightly in volume, then stop abruptly*	(Page 54)
Cue 20	After **Clem** puts pad on wound under jacket *Car starts, revs up violently, and roars away*	(Page 55)
Cue 21	**Hester:** "It's too late." *First loud-hailer speech starts*	(Page 57)
Cue 22	**Joe:** "... don't want to remember." *Second loud-hailer speech starts*	(Page 58)
Cue 23	**Joe** stands in doorway with light on face *Third loud-hailer speech starts*	(Page 58)

SHEPHERDS' DANCE Edward German (in two parts but can be sung in unison if wished)

This text by W G Rothery is reprinted by kind permission of Novello & Company Ltd

Tempo Imo

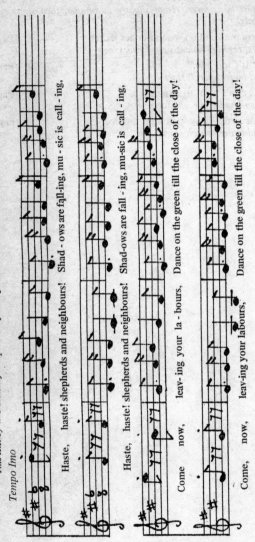

JUDAS MACCABEUS Handel
This extract is fom the tenor solo. Julia can start on any note to suit her own voice.